Creative
Expression
Activities
for Teens

Creative Expression Activities for Teens

Exploring Identity through Art, Craft and Journaling

Bonnie Thomas

Jessica Kingsley Publishers
London and Philadelphia

First published in 2011
by Jessica Kingsley Publishers
116 Pentonville Road
London N1 9JB, UK
and
400 Market Street, Suite 400
Philadelphia, PA 19106, USA

www.jkp.com

Library of Congress Cataloging in Publication Data
A CIP catalog record for this book is available from the Library of Congress

British Library Cataloguing in Publication Data
A CIP catalogue record for this book is available from the British Library

ISBN 978 1 84905 842 1

Printed and bound in Great Britain by
MPG Books Group Limited

Contents

Introduction 9
Creative Hunting and Gathering 11

Part I Art Projects and Creative Challenges 15

Artist Trading Cards (ATCs) and Art Cards, Editions, and
    Originals (ACEOs) 17
Altered Books 20
Photojournalism 23
Me, Myself, and I—Three Building Blocks 24
Body Art 27
My Personal Totem 28
A Metaphorical Family Tree 30
Life Map 33
Mini Shrines 35
A Tribute to Imaginary Friends 38
Childhood Survival 101 40
Letter to Your Child Self 42
Secrets with Wings 44
Personal Mantras 46
Mandalas 48
Mixed Media Self-Portraits 50
Themed Family Portraits 53
Rites of Passage Passport 54
Emo Dolls 56
Recurring Dreams 58

My Happy Place   *60*

Shadowboxing   *61*

Put Your Stamp on It   *63*

Inspiration Decks   *66*

Super Easy Accessories   *68*

Triptychs   *70*

Paper Chains   *72*

Art in Unexpected Places   *75*

Tribute to a Special Memory   *78*

Part II Journaling   **81**

Autobiography in Metaphors   *83*

A Kaleidoscope of Friends   *85*

Snapshot Moments   *86*

Comic Life   *87*

Mini Graphic Novels   *88*

Wishes   *90*

The Ultimate Day   *92*

Freedom From   *93*

Rites of Passage Plan   *95*

Hilarious Haikus   *97*

Venting in Gibberish   *98*

Part III Miniature Projects for Personal Spaces   **99**

Bedroom Pop Art   *101*

Wooden Drawer Pulls   *102*

Light Switch Covers   *103*

Mini Memo Boards and Corkboards   *104*

Altered Pushpins and Thumbtacks   *105*

Altered Clothespins and Hang Line   *106*

Magnets   *107*

Key Chains   *108*

Altered Tin Containers   *109*

Mini Flag Banners   *110*

Moustache Pencil Toppers   *111*

**Part IV Incorporating the Activities into
          Treatment—A Section for Counselors   113**

Developing a Therapeutic Alliance with Your Client   *115*

*Mood Disorders, Anxiety Disorders, and General Coping
    Skills*   *116*

Family Dynamics and Family Roles   *120*

Attention Deficit Disorders   *121*

*Disruptive Behavior Disorders and Oppositional Defiant
    Disorder*   *123*

Substance Use/Abuse   *125*

Dissociative Disorders   *128*

Gender Identity Disorders   *131*

Adjustment Disorders and Grief   *133*

Trauma   *137*

Introduction

"Adolescence" is a word that strikes fear in many. It has a reputation for being tumultuous, heart wrenching, and wrought with growing pains of all sorts. But in spite of the emotional upheavals and the day-to-day challenges of teen life, adolescence is a beautiful transformation from child to adult. Yes, I said beautiful.

And yes, I meant it.

Over the years I have worked with adolescents in various settings—in psychiatric hospitals; in a public housing neighborhood program; in schools; and in juvenile detention settings. If there is one thing I have learned, is that teens have a lot to express. They are constantly thinking, feeling, and getting caught up in each and every moment (past, present, and future) all at once…but not so good communicating about it. Good communication is a challenge for even the most eloquent and self-assured adults, so how can we help foster good communication in teens?

Words are not always enough. There are times when people need something more to express their deepest most vulnerable thoughts and feelings. This is where art and creative expression comes in—it is the perfect companion for teens. Art and creative expression can unleash a whirlwind of emotion; it can say what words cannot.

The projects and activities in this book are all designed to address the need for expression. If you are a teen reading this book, dive in and try the activities that appeal to you. If you are a professional who works with teens (such as a counselor, youth group leader, or group home facilitator) then review the activities and see which ones fit your client's needs best. Part IV of this book is specially included for counselors and shows how to incorporate these activities into treatment plans.

The activities in this book are appropriate for people ages 13 and older. Each and every activity touches upon a part of the Self (past, present, and future) and gives the artist an opportunity to express a little or a lot about him/herself. However, if you (the person doing the activities in this book) suffer from any mental health issues and/or have a trauma history, it is best to use caution in which activities you choose. If any of these activities bring up feelings that are uncomfortable to you, please tell an adult or seek help from a professional.

Creative Hunting
and Gathering

Creative Hunting and Gathering is a precursor to the activities that follow in this book. Why? First, this activity is designed to jump start your inspiration. Second, any items that you gather in this activity can be used in several activities in this book.

You will need:

- a large envelope or box to hold any items you find.

Go on a scavenger hunt of sorts and collect little things that appeal to you—here are some ideas to get you started:

- Flip through some magazines and cut out any phrases or pictures that inspire you.

- Take photographs of your environment (school, neighborhood, bedroom, etc.) that you find interesting, inspiring, beautiful, or curious.

- Gather some photos of favorite memories or from special occasions that you were especially proud of, e.g. a picture of the time you participated in a competition.

- Go to a hardware or paint store and browse through the paint samples. Many of these places allow you to take samples for free (please ask first). Gather some samples of colors you love. You can also collect a few samples that have color names you like as well.

- Photocopy a favorite or special recipe.

- Collect any fun little items that you enjoy looking at or holding in your hand:

  o buttons

  o trinkets

  o shells

  o stones

  o tiny toys, e.g. gumball machine finds

  o fortunes from a fortune cookie

  o bubble gum or candy wrappers from a favorite candy

  o patterned paper you enjoy

  o ribbon

  o special beads and charms

  o bottle caps

  o found objects, e.g. washers, watch parts, cabochons

  o a puzzle piece

  o a key

  o a product label, e.g. cut out a favorite design from a tea box

  o parts from broken jewelry

  o game pieces

  o cards from a card deck (playing cards, tarot cards, skill cards, etc.)

- favorite doodles from your school notebook (if you're a doodler)

- saved postage stamps

- special notes or cards from friends and family

- travel mementos, e.g. postcards or souvenirs.

• Take a photograph of a local place you find intriguing, relaxing, or inspiring.

• Get a brochure or pictures from a travel agency or travel website of someplace you would love to travel.

At the end of this time you will have a collection of items that inspire you, captivate you, and/or make you feel happy. If you enjoyed this process, continue to add to your list and collection as time goes on.

PART I

Art Projects and Creative Challenges

◇◇◇◇◇◇◇◇◇◇◇◇◇◇◇◇◇◇◇◇◇◇◇◇◇◇◇◇◇◇◇

The following activities in this section of the book are designed for creative expression. There are no right or wrong ways to create ANYTHING in this book. These activities are here to inspire and guide, but not to dictate. You are the artist—you are the creator.

Artist Trading Cards (ATCs) and Art Cards, Editions, and Originals (ACEOs)

♦ ♦ ♦ ♦ ♦ ♦ ♦ ♦ ♦ ♦ ♦ ♦ ♦ ♦ ♦ ♦ ♦ ♦ ♦ ♦

Artist Trading Cards have become an international phenomenon in artistic self-expression—they are works of art that people create on card stock or other sturdy paper measuring 2½ x 3½ inches (64 x 89 mm). Creators of ATCs trade their works of art from across the globe to right in their neighborhoods—many communities even have local meet-ups to trade their ATCs, and there are also online trading sites where you can trade around the world.

Art Cards, Editions, and Originals are quite similar in style to ATCs except ACEOs are created to be sold and collected, rather than traded.

There are many resources available to ACEO and ATC artists online. If this project inspires you, you can run a search online using keywords "Artist Trading Cards" and "Art Cards, Editions, and Originals". You can find such information as the history of this style of art; contests where you can submit your work; local gatherings of like-minded artists; and techniques for creating such cards.

Many art stores and websites also sell cards specifically for ATCs. However, you can easily use playing cards and other recycled materials, or simply cut out your own cards using the designated measurements.

Now that you know what ATCs and ACEOs are, try creating some! The possibilities are practically endless—create any form of miniature artwork on a card sized 2½ x 3½ inches (64 x 89 mm).

Some ideas to get you started:

- Cover your card with newsprint and then sketch a picture on the newsprint using charcoal or colored pencil.

- Cover your card with sheet music and then add some collage materials over it.

- Choose a theme for your card, e.g. a fairy tale; mermaids; coffee shops; graphic novel art; trees; angels; junk food; or insects.

- Create a series of ATCs related to one theme—this is a great way to delve into a subject area and interpret it from many creative angles. Here are some series ideas to get you started:

  - Create several ATCs of favorite characters from a book, such as *Alice in Wonderland*.

  - Devote a series of ATCs to color themes.

  - Design a series of ATCs that evokes different emotions.

  - Make an entire deck of ACEOs for creative game playing or fun fortune telling. See the Inspiration Decks section for more deck ideas (p.66).

An assortment of Artist Trading Cards.

Altered Books

♦ ♦ ♦ ♦ ♦ ♦ ♦ ♦ ♦ ♦ ♦ ♦ ♦ ♦ ♦ ♦ ♦

Altered books are works of art created from recycled books of any kind. Here are two examples:

- Books can be re-used as scrapbooks and memory books—the pages are simply used as the backdrop for each page.

- Children's board books can easily be transformed into altered works of art—the sturdy pages hold up well to added artwork and embellishments. Plus, they usually have a limited number of pages to work with. These books are perfect for creating your own stories (such as altered fairy tales or mini graphic novels).

Books have also been turned into everything from hidden compartments to purses, so if this is a project that inspires you, turn to the internet where resources are abundant for altered book projects.

Where to find books to alter:

- Perhaps the easiest way to find books that are no longer wanted is by simply asking your parents or extended family members (grandparents, aunts, uncles, etc.). Let them know the book will be completely altered so they are clear what you are using it for. Or you yourself may have some books you no longer need or want.

- If your town or city has a recycling center you may be able to check there. Some recycling centers allow for people to come and take materials—some even have an area for leaving goods that are still useable. Books are a common find at these places.

- Yard sales, tag sales, flea markets, and antique shops are great for finding a particular book. For example, my favorite books to alter tend to be vintage hardcover texts full of interesting pages—sheet music, poetry, or foreign languages.

Once you find your book, decide what you will use it for and how you will alter it. If you decide to leave the pages "as is," then you have a head start. If you need to prep the pages for paint or collage materials, you may need to sand the pages lightly with sandpaper and/or apply a light base coat of a primer like gesso (e.g. if you are working with a child's board book or hardcover).

Some fun alterations you can add to your book:

- Fold some of the pages into interesting angles or shapes to add depth and dimension to your book.

- Tear out some pages from your book to create envelopes that can be glued back onto other pages inside the book (put something inside the envelope for the reader to find).

- Use collage on one page, sketches on another—mix it up.

- Watercolor crayons can be used to sketch, outline, or shade in areas of your pages. Use a paintbrush to brush a light amount of water over these areas for added color. Allow to dry.

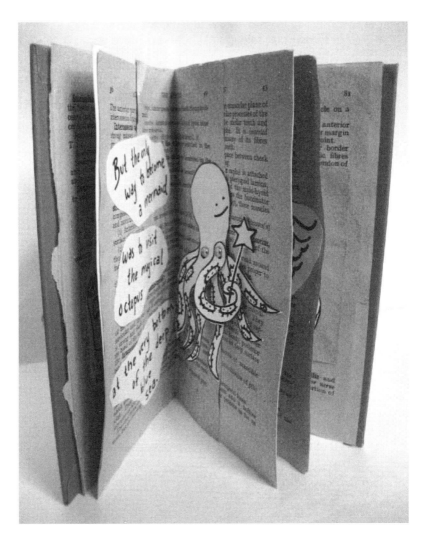

This book was created by removing pages from a small hardcover book and then working with the few pages left intact. Scraps of paper from a vintage anatomy book were glued onto the pages and then paper dolls were partially glued in for illustrations.

Photojournalism

♦ ♦ ♦ ♦ ♦ ♦ ♦ ♦ ♦ ♦ ♦ ♦ ♦ ♦ ♦ ♦ ♦ ♦ ♦

Take photos that represent a part of your life or a day in your life and then use them in a piece of art. You could use the altered book format to display your photos; create a collage with the photos; or glue them into a journal. You can be as creative as you like!

Examples of Photojournal themes:

- My friend's shoes

- My friend's lockers

- Cars my friends ride in

- Things that catch my eye on the way to school

- Graffiti in my town

- The strange things my friends and I eat for breakfast.

Me, Myself, and I—Three Building Blocks

♦ ♦ ♦ ♦ ♦ ♦ ♦ ♦ ♦ ♦ ♦ ♦ ♦ ♦ ♦ ♦ ♦ ♦ ♦

Create a set of three building blocks that define who you are, or express something about you.

You will need:

- three wooden blocks—these can be plain wooden blocks (purchased from a craft store) or recycled wooden blocks (e.g. toy blocks)
- sandpaper.

You may need:

- paint
- permanent markers
- paper
- colored pencils
- collage images
- Mod Podge, collage glue, or varnish.

First, create a theme for your building blocks such as:

- Things that fill my heart with joy
- Past, Present, and Future
- Things I am hoping for or working towards

- Challenges in my life

- People and passions that have inspired me

- Friends and family that support who I am

- Brief quotes/song lyrics I like

- Artwork I love

- No theme at all—just doodles and random stuff.

Second, prepare the blocks if you need to:

- Do your blocks need to be sanded? If you are using children's toy blocks, please be sure they are lead-free before sanding.

- You can choose to paint the block surfaces; cut out paper squares to glue on; or leave plain before adding words or art.

Third, add artwork and/or words to your blocks. If you want to give your work an aged look you can sand the block surfaces, or just sand the block edges. When the blocks are complete you can choose to seal the blocks with varnish or collage glue, like Mod Podge.

When completed, the blocks can be a standing piece of art for a shelf, window sill, or bureau. You can arrange and rearrange the blocks to fit your mood or to remind you of something important (for example, if you created blocks with the theme of "things that fill my heart with joy," you can place your blocks nearby to remind you of these things during a particularly rough day or week).

These blocks were created using plain wooden blocks from a craft store and painted. Paper images were cut out and glued onto the blocks.

Body Art

♦ ♦ ♦ ♦ ♦ ♦ ♦ ♦ ♦ ♦ ♦ ♦ ♦ ♦ ♦ ♦ ♦ ♦ ♦ ♦

I am going to keep this section short and sweet—buy some washable tattoo markers and create some art on your body. Doodle, draw, zig-zag, squiggle, polka dot, and funny face your way to a new you. Draw towns and cities up and down your arms...create new solar systems and alien life forms on your ankles...draw faces on your fingertips...draw moustaches on your face. Just ask your parents first so I don't get in trouble.

My Personal Totem

♦ ♦ ♦ ♦ ♦ ♦ ♦ ♦ ♦ ♦ ♦ ♦ ♦ ♦ ♦ ♦ ♦ ♦ ♦ ♦

A totem is usually a symbol or group of symbols that represent a family, tribe, or clan. In this project, however, a totem will be created to serve as an emblem of who YOU are.

If you have the time and interest in doing a little research, you can look online at "totem animals" and what these animals represent. Choose one or more animals for yourself. For example, one animal could represent an animal guide helping you through whichever stage of life you are in right now; another animal could represent an inner strength of yours or personality trait. You can also choose a group of animals to represent the totem animals you believe have been with you throughout your life. For example, perhaps as a child you had a bear as a totem animal and now in your adult life you have an owl. Your finished art piece could be a tribute to all of the animal guides you've ever had.

Next, design your totem. It can be in any art form you choose. Some creative suggestions:

- Draw, sketch or trace a traditional totem pole based on the animals you chose.

- Use the actual words of the totem animals in a piece of art.

- Create a diorama using plastic animals to represent the totem animals.

- Make a mini shrine of your totem animals. See Mini Shrines section (p.35).

- Create a necklace that has beads or charms of your totem animals included in it.

The names of the totem animals were used in this piece.

A Metaphorical Family Tree

Traditional Family Trees are usually charts on paper that map out who your parents, siblings, and grandparents are (some family trees map several generations of family, where others are succinct). In this project, however, you can create a completely different type of family tree—A Metaphorical Family Tree.

Before you create your tree, it helps to get a visual of it. Let's start with the "Tree" itself. If you had to describe your family as a tree, what kind of tree would they be? Here are some metaphors to think about:

- What kind of tree is it? These are some examples of how a person MIGHT choose a tree to fit their family—if you do a little research on the internet about trees, you might find a tree that fits your family makeup.

    - An oak tree might symbolize a solid, well-balanced family.

    - A weeping willow might symbolize a sad, grieving, or depressed family.

    - A redwood tree might symbolize a domineering family, or family with a lot of power in the community.

    - A Japanese maple might symbolize a family that is fragile and needs a lot of special attention and care.

    - A grafted tree might represent an adoptive family.

- Is the tree healthy? Strong? Weak?

- Does the tree live in a warm climate or a cold climate? Does it live where the weather changes a lot? And how well does the tree tolerate these changes?

- Is the tree well taken care of or is it undernourished?

The branches of the tree will represent you, siblings, and parents or guardians. You choose where the branches go:

- If someone is quiet, shy, or ignored in the family, they may be a branch that is hard to see.

- If there is a chronically ill family member the branch may look unhealthy.

- If someone is a nurturing person in the family, s/he might have a nest on their branch.

- A baby or young child in the family might have a smaller branch. An older member in the family might have acorns, seeds, or fruit on its limbs.

You can even symbolize the person's character by what kind of bird is perched on its branch:

- An owl might sit on a wise person's branch.

- A woodpecker might sit on the branch of someone who is interfering, nosy, or constantly bugging you.

- A vulture might sit on the branch of someone who is predatory or waiting to do harm.

- A dove might sit on a branch of someone who is a peacekeeper in the family.

You get to define who your family is in this project. If you decide to do more than one tree that's okay too. Some teens I have worked with decided to do step families on separate trees or do their biological family separate from an adoptive family. Remember, you are the artist!

Okay, so now that you have thought through all of these possibilities, design your own family tree using any medium.

Creative suggestions:

- Sculpt or create a 3-D family tree.

- Use a jewelry tree or decorative tree and hang ornaments or charms from the tree representing the various family members.

- Use the traditional template for a family tree but choose a picture of an archetypal figure or character to go along with the names—the picture is meant to be a representation of a characteristic that person shares with the character. Here are some examples: a fairy godmother; a witch; the grim reaper; a princess; a clown.

- Veto the whole idea of using your own family and instead, create who you WISH had been your family. You have absolute creative freedom in this exercise.

A diorama of two family trees. The parents are divorced. The children are represented by glass beads on the trees.

Life Map

♦ ♦ ♦ ♦ ♦ ♦ ♦ ♦ ♦ ♦ ♦ ♦ ♦ ♦ ♦ ♦ ♦ ♦ ♦

Create a map representing where you have been in your life and where you are going. This can be a metaphorical map or a traditional map.

Creative suggestions:

- Create a "legend" for your map. Different landmarks can represent different metaphors:

    ○ Bridges might represent places in your life where you recovered from a traumatic event or "crossed over" to a new life (for better or worse).

    ○ Dead ends might represent times in your life where you expected something to happen, but it never came to fruition.

    ○ Mountains and mountain ranges could be problems and/or obstacles you overcame or are still facing.

    ○ Lighthouses can represent safe havens from stormy moments in your life.

    ○ Caves and haunted forests can symbolize moments in your life that felt dark and lonely.

    ○ Completely blackened out areas can represent moments in your life you are not able or ready to work through yet.

- Create a pirate map. Use buried treasure chests to represent places in your life where you have "buried" certain parts of yourself, secrets, or memories.

- Create a compass rose for your map. What do North, East, South, and West represent to you? Which direction is the compass rose guiding you?

A traditional Life Map.

Mini Shrines

♦ ♦ ♦ ♦ ♦ ♦ ♦ ♦ ♦ ♦ ♦ ♦ ♦ ♦ ♦ ♦ ♦ ♦ ♦

Shrines are collections of items that pay respect to a person or place. For example, some people create shrines in memory of someone that has passed away. Some shrines are created for good luck or good fortune. Other shrines are created for religious purposes.

Mini Shrines are attractive for their portability (some are even small enough to fit in a pocket). They can be little reminders of who you are, something you love, or good luck to have with you on an important day.

The Mini Shrines in this activity can be created using small containers such as recycled mint tins and matchboxes. I prefer to use recycled containers but mint tins and matchboxes can be purchased new at craft stores, and even grocery stores (the matchboxes I am referring to are the ones with the slide out tray).

First, decide on a theme for your shrine:

- Will your shrine be for good luck?

- Will it be dedicated to the memory of a person, pet, or item you no longer have in your life?

- Will it be a shrine for inspiration?

- Will it be dedicated to someone famous who has inspired you?

- How about a Mini Zen Garden? All you need is a mini tin, sand, and some rocks.

- Perhaps you can make a shrine for someone else, such as a Get Well shrine.

Next, choose and prepare your container.

- If you are using a tin:

    o Wash it out with soap and water and make sure it has dried thoroughly before using it.

    o Lightly sand the areas of the tin where you will be applying any paint, glue, or paper.

    o Use acrylic paint for painting any area. Mod Podge works well for decoupage or gluing on paper.

- If using a matchbox, you may want to paint the inside tray using acrylic paint. You can also paint the cover of the matchbox or simply wrap the outside in decorative paper. Allow the matchbox to dry.

Add any artwork as needed to embellish and decorate the shrine:

- pictures and quotes cut out from magazines

- mini sketches or drawings you have created

- meaningful words

- ribbons, stickers, and beads can be glued and sealed in place.

Last, add some parts to the shrine that are removable and/or interactive if you like:

- charms

- talismans

- bottle caps (images can be glued inside)

- tiny notes or scrolls with words of wisdom

- fortunes from a fortune cookie or bubble gum wrapper

- magnets for the tin shrines (see p.107 for instructions on making your own magnets)

- folded paper, accordion-style, can fit into matchboxes to create mini books or pop-outs.

A variety of mini shrines for various uses.

A Tribute to
Imaginary Friends

◆ ◆ ◆ ◆ ◆ ◆ ◆ ◆ ◆ ◆ ◆ ◆ ◆ ◆ ◆ ◆ ◆ ◆ ◆

Did you have imaginary friends when you were little? Children create imaginary friends for many reasons. If you were one of these children, why did you create YOUR imaginary friend/s? What purpose did they serve? Whatever reason you created them, your imaginary friends are worth honoring—they shared important moments in your life, both good and bad, right alongside with you. Create a piece of art that pays tribute to your imaginary friend/s from childhood.

Creative suggestions:

- Create a shrine or diorama that has an artistic representation of your imaginary friends included.

- Write the imaginary friend/s a thank-you letter using your non-dominant hand to write it.

- Create an art doll that represents one or more of your imaginary friends. See Emo Doll section for ideas on making a variety of art dolls (p.56).

- Draw a portrait of you and your imaginary friend/s.

- Create a multi-medium picture or sculpture of your imaginary friend/s.

Find a place to display or hang your artwork—admire and honor your creativity as a creator.

A diorama paying tribute to imaginary friends.

Childhood Survival 101

♦ ♦ ♦ ♦ ♦ ♦ ♦ ♦ ♦ ♦ ♦ ♦ ♦ ♦ ♦ ♦ ♦ ♦ ♦

I am always amazed as a counselor to hear what people survived as children and teens. From injuries, to unsupervised moments, to trauma and illnesses…it seems many people have at least one "survival" moment in their childhood. Take a mental note of all of the accomplishments you made as a child—all that you survived and endured. The survival moment can be however you define it—and understandably this can be a difficult subject. Be gentle with yourself, breathe deep, and give honor and love to yourself throughout this activity. Create a piece of art that pays tribute to this child and what s/he experienced (or may still be experiencing).

Creative suggestions:

- If you believe in guardian angels, create a piece of art that pays tribute to your own.

- Design a piece of art that represents you "leaving behind" a part of your life that was challenging. Will you be walking away from it? Burying it? Honoring it?

- Create a book, poem, mini graphic novel or story about your less-than-perfect childhood experiences with titles like:

  ○ "Horrendous Babysitters/Nannies I Survived—A Tragicomedy in 3 Acts"

  ○ "My ABCs of Near Death Experiences"

  ○ "I Didn't Do It. Okay, Yes I Did"

- o "10 Things I Learned All on My Own"

- o "How I Survived Algebra—My Many Doodles"

- o "Summer Camp and Separation Anxiety"

- o "Tales of Terror—Living with Sisters/Brothers"

- o "School Lunches I Ate and Lived to Tell About".

A large matchbox with sliding tray was used to create this "house." Inside are figurines, and the child figurine looks out the window. The window to the outside world is her inspiration for survival.

Letter to Your Child Self

♦ ♦ ♦ ♦ ♦ ♦ ♦ ♦ ♦ ♦ ♦ ♦ ♦ ♦ ♦ ♦ ♦

Write a letter to your child self telling you what you needed to know, or what you needed to hear from someone you looked up to. You can write this letter from the voice of your older self, as a guardian angel, as a mentor, or wise soul, etc.

Create a piece of art around this letter. The letter itself can be altered as needed to fit your emotional and artistic needs.

Creative suggestions:

- If you are familiar with digital art, you could photograph your letter and superimpose it into the hands of a childhood picture of yourself.

- Write the letter, burn it, and use the ashes within a piece of art (okay, I know you are teenagers so legally I have to tell you to exercise caution here and ask for adult supervision if you are going to burn anything).

- Place your letter in a secret compartment within the art. For example, if you are using a collage medium, the letter could be tucked into an envelope and added to the collage arrangement.

- Turn your letter into a paper mache bowl:
    - Tear your letter into thin strips.
    - Use a disposable paper bowl as a frame for your paper mache bowl.

o Mix flour and warm water in a separate container until the mixture is the consistency of glue. Smooth out any lumps.

o Dip the paper strips into the flour/water mixture and remove any excess goo—sliding the strip of paper between two fingers usually does the trick.

o Lay the strip of paper over the paper bowl. Repeat this pattern until the bowl has one layer of paper mache strips over it. Allow it to dry.

o Repeat the paper mache process until your bowl has enough layers on it to be as sturdy as you wish it to be. You will most likely run out of paper strips from your letter. This is okay—just use newspaper strips or paper towel strips to complete the bowl.

o When your bowl is complete, paint it with acrylic paints and seal it with a varnish or sealant.

o Display your bowl someplace special. You will most likely be the only person who knows how amazingly sacred and special this bowl is. You can fill your bowl with mini inspiration cards (see Inspiration Decks, p.66) or use it as a place to put your keys, rings, or jewelry.

This bowl was created using paper mache and strips of paper from the letter.

Secrets with Wings

◆ ◆ ◆ ◆ ◆ ◆ ◆ ◆ ◆ ◆ ◆ ◆ ◆ ◆ ◆ ◆ ◆ ◆ ◆ ◆

This project is a personal favorite. I hear many clients tell me day in and day out that the emotional load of carrying secrets from childhood and/or their teen years is a burden and feels "yucky." Yet, sometimes it is beyond the person's ability or timing to say what those secrets are. This activity is a creative way to release some of this emotional load without exposing the actual secret.

For this project, therefore, you will create a piece of art that has a secret from your childhood or present life hidden in the finished product.

However you choose to represent the secret in this activity is fine. It does not have to be written out or "told"—it can be represented metaphorically.

Creative suggestions:

- Create a figurine representing yourself—this can be made from polymer clay (e.g. Sculpey or Fimo) or self-hardening clay. You can actually write your secret on a teeny tiny piece of paper and place it in your figurine as you create it. Follow the directions for completing the figurine per the clay guidelines (many have to be baked). The figurine can be the final product or it can be used in a broader piece of art (e.g. a figurine within a diorama).

- If you can sew, create a quilt or smaller quilted art piece that has the secret stitched within it. Again, the actual words do not need to be obvious; the secret can be coded or expressed in metaphorical pictures or patterns.

- Make a paper mache bowl and use the strip/s of paper as part of the material used to make the bowl. See directions to make a paper mache bowl in the Letter to Your Child Self section (p.42).

This piece of art is actually contained inside a glass jar. The tree in the center is actually the "secret"—the secret was written on paper and then formed into a cone shape. Paper mache was applied to the cone to strengthen it. The tree was then covered in glue and sprinkled with glitter. The girl standing in front of the tree is guarding her secret.

Personal Mantras

♦ ♦ ♦ ♦ ♦ ♦ ♦ ♦ ♦ ♦ ♦ ♦ ♦ ♦ ♦ ♦ ♦ ♦ ♦ ♦

Do you ever forget to take deep breaths, or forget to think of the positive, or need reminding now and then to practice self-care?

Think of your own Personal Mantra—something you need reminding about each day, or when things get rough. Make sure it is a phrase that is kind or nurturing to your heart and soul. Here are some examples of mantras:

- I take deep cleansing breaths.
- Breathe in love, breathe out anger.
- Stretch.
- I deserve happiness.
- Think positive.
- Laugh.
- I am important.
- I am strong.
- I can do this.

Next, turn this mantra into a piece of art. Here are some creative suggestions:

- Create a painting or collage that has your Personal Mantra in it. Frame and hang this where you will see it.

- Use markers for windows/glass to decorate your bathroom mirror with your personal mantra. Each morning you can start your day with a reminder of your mantra.

- Use shrinking plastic or a laminate/countertop sample (found at hardware stores) to write your mantra on. Attach this to a key ring and add it to your keys. You will have a portable mantra.

- Create an ATC or ACEO with your personal mantra on it (see the section on Artist Trading Cards, p.17). Laminate the finished piece of art and then keep it in your wallet or purse.

- Purchase unfinished wood letters to spell out a simple mantra such as "Breathe" or "Calm." Decorate the letters using collage or paint and then hang them on your wall.

- Create a bracelet using letter beads to spell out a one-word mantra.

- If you enjoy reading, create a bookmark with your mantra on it.

A collection of personal mantras in various mediums.

Mandalas

◆ ◆ ◆ ◆ ◆ ◆ ◆ ◆ ◆ ◆ ◆ ◆ ◆ ◆ ◆ ◆ ◆ ◆ ◆

Mandalas are symbolic pieces of art that have been around for centuries. They are typically circular, symmetrical and used to aid in meditation and focus. Mandalas are easily found on the internet and can be quite calming to color. However, in this activity you are going to create your own mandala.

First, find something circular that you can trace, e.g. the bottom of a coffee can or cereal bowl.

Next, focus on a theme for your mandala:

- The theme can be a color or color scheme:
    - Earth colors
    - Water colors
    - Fire colors
    - Rainbow colors
- The theme can be a repeated design or pattern:
    - Swirls
    - Flowers
    - Leaves
    - Waves
    - Polka dots
    - Peace signs
    - Doodles
    - Rainbows
    - Hearts
- The theme can be a feeling, such as bliss, rage, or melancholy.

Use a pencil to sketch a design within the mandala that relates back to your theme—do not worry about symmetry for this activity.

When you are pleased with the design, add some color. You can outline the details of your mandala first in permanent black ink if that helps, then fill in the colors with colored pencils or markers.

What can you do with your mandala?

- Display it/hang it up on a wall or in your locker.

- Decorate a book protector with it for one of your school books.

- Create a book of black-and-white mandalas for someone to color, like a friend, younger sibling, or even yourself. Just remember to keep the original/s and photocopy the mandalas for coloring.

A mandala shown in black and white before color was applied.

Mixed Media Self-Portraits

♦ ♦ ♦ ♦ ♦ ♦ ♦ ♦ ♦ ♦ ♦ ♦ ♦ ♦ ♦ ♦ ♦ ♦ ♦

Create a portrait or sculpture of yourself using a combination of art mediums. There are many materials to choose from when creating mixed media art—anything from the traditional supplies to the unexpected.

- Create a self-portrait using collage. Collages can be paper materials combined together to create a piece of art (e.g. magazine pictures, newspaper, scrapbook paper, etc.). But collages can also incorporate other materials, such as charms, ribbons, favorite tea labels, candy wrappers, fortunes, notes from friends, bottle caps, doodles cut from your class notes, buttons, and other items that appeal to you. Here are two examples of collages you can do for a self-portrait:

  - Find a large piece of foam board or poster board. Create a collage about yourself using items that reflect on your personality, passions, preferences, and philosophies. These can be placed around the board as a layout, rather than an actual portrait. Include pictures of things that evoke emotion in you; textures that appeal to you; labels from food that has been part of a memorable experience; music lyrics; quotes; words you love; and any other items you can attach to the collage that have meaning to you. To finish off the collage, decorate or outline the border to give it some added definition and visual appeal. You can even hang more collage items from the bottom of the board if you like—charms, flags, beaded ribbons, and more can be further added for embellishment.

o   Draw an outline of yourself or part of your self, such as the face. Fill in the details of the picture using paper items for your collage material. You could cut out actual eyes, ears, nose, and lips from a magazine. You could also cut out skin tones from magazines as the first layer of your collage. This could create the "skin" on your face. Then sketch or collage over this layer with any details and facial features. Words can even be cut from magazines to be the defining lines of your body and features. The words can be chosen to add even more to the self-portrait concept; for example, the word "strength" might outline the nose, or the word "beauty" might create an eyebrow.

- Decorate and/or embellish an existing box or container so that it is a representation of you (physically or metaphorically). Then fill the box with things that you enjoy or things that describe and define who you are.

- Draw a self-portrait with crayon or oil pastel and then paint over it with watercolors. The watercolors won't penetrate where you have drawn, which creates a unique look for your picture.

- Sketch a self-portrait on a recycled piece of paper, such as a newspaper, sheet music, homework assignment, or cereal box.

- Create a diorama with yourself portrayed in it. You can choose a pre-existing figurine to represent yourself and then create a diorama scene around it. Remember, the figurine doesn't have to be a person; the figurine can be any metaphorical representation of yourself. You can also create a figurine of yourself using clay and then create your diorama around the clay figurine.

- Create a drawing of yourself and cut it out. Attach wings to the drawing of yourself (can be drawn wings; metal charm wings; wings cut from a photo of a butterfly) and then use this figure in a piece of art.

This self-portrait was created using recycled goods found at a recycling center. Broken doll parts were wired together for the head and torso. A dress was created from an old flower arrangement tool. The dress is also a bird cage—there are two little bird charms that hang inside.

Themed Family Portraits

Choose a theme for a family portrait and then create a picture of your family based on it. Here are some ideas to try:

- My family…as fairy tale characters
- My family…as superheroes and villains
- My family…as buildings in a town
- My family…as plants
- My family…as types of candy
- My family…as mythical creatures
- My family…as tarot cards
- My family…as books on a library shelf
- My family…as crayons

Rites of Passage Passport

♦ ♦ ♦ ♦ ♦ ♦ ♦ ♦ ♦ ♦ ♦ ♦ ♦ ♦ ♦ ♦ ♦ ♦ ♦ ♦

Brainstorm a list of what you want to accomplish in your lifetime. Include achievements you hope to reach or places you want to travel. Here are some examples:

- graduating high school and/or college
- working in a dream job
- making a certain salary
- owning a home
- getting a license to drive or fly
- finding a partner or getting married
- running for office or getting elected for a political position
- publishing a book
- overcoming a fear or phobia
- traveling to a certain place
- making a difference in the world by joining a cause or participating in social change
- owning a vehicle
- reaching sobriety for a certain amount of time
- finding your voice to speak from the heart
- fun personal goals like "To go on a zip line in the rainforest".

Next, create a mini booklet in the style of a passport. This can be as simple as cutting some standard white printer paper in half; then folding these pages in half to create a book. You can choose a different colored cardstock paper for the cover.

Put a goal on each page of your passport. You can choose to leave some pages empty in case you want to add to it later.

Decorate the pages of your book if you like—they can be painted, sketched, collaged, or embellished.

Each time you accomplish a goal or complete a rite of passage, commemorate it in your "passport." You could stamp the page, or add a small memento to it (e.g. a stamp from a country you visited; your college ID card after you graduate; or a photocopy of your first paycheck at a dream job).

Keep your passport with you as you move through adulthood. Even if you never add to your book, you might come across it later in life and look back at the dream and goals you had at the age you are now. You may find you have accomplished a few of your goals, changed your mind about others, or are still working to achieve some of them.

Two Rites of Passage Passport booklets.

Emo Dolls

◆ ◆ ◆ ◆ ◆ ◆ ◆ ◆ ◆ ◆ ◆ ◆ ◆ ◆ ◆ ◆ ◆ ◆

I don't know why I love these, but I do. Emo Dolls are simply dolls created to show emotion—typically sad, moody, brooding emotions. However, since you are the artist, you can create your own Emo Dolls to be whatever emotion you desire them to be. Creative suggestions:

- Some craft shops sell plain muslin dolls that are pre-made (these are especially convenient for people like myself who lack sewing skills). You can purchase these dolls and decorate them or alter them yourself. You can draw on them with fabric markers; sew embellishments on them; add string for hair; or even paint them with fabric paint.

- If you can sew, you can create and design your own Emo Dolls—they can be as primitive or elaborate as you like. Try mixing fabric patterns and colors to evoke emotion in your dolls. Stitch expressive faces on them.

- Create some paper Emo Dolls:

  - These can be created in traditional paper doll style where the body, head, and limbs are attached with brads (mini split-pin paper fasteners). Brads come in many sizes and colors, but the tiny brads work best for paper dolls.

  - Expand on the paper doll theme by using a new medium for the body of your Emo Doll. For example, use a matchbox for the body and attach paper limbs and a paper head using brads and a hole punch. Matchboxes are especially fun to use as bodies because you can further alter the inside of the matchbox to hide "secrets": quotes; lucky charms; or other small trinkets.

- Create some wooden Emo Dolls. Many craft shops sell wood people figurines (sometimes under the label of "game pieces"). These can be turned into Emo Dolls using paint, permanent markers, or colored pencils. You can also glue string (for hair) and paper items onto these dolls for added detail. See what kinds of emotions you can express using these wooden figurines.

- Create an entire collection of Emo Dolls and/or trade them with friends.

These Emo Dolls were created using pre-made muslin dolls from a craft store.

Recurring Dreams

♦ ♦ ♦ ♦ ♦ ♦ ♦ ♦ ♦ ♦ ♦ ♦ ♦ ♦ ♦ ♦ ♦ ♦ ♦

Do you have any recurring dreams, or one recurring dream in particular? If so, what do you think the underlying message to the dream is? If you are not sure, it may help to look up dream symbols/dream interpretations online or in many of the books devoted to the meaning of dreams. Create a piece of art that speaks to a theme in a recurring dream you have had.

Creative suggestions:

- If you are not aware of any recurring themes or symbols in your dreams, start a dream journal (or add a dream journal section to your already existing journal). Keep the journal next to your place of sleep with a writing utensil and book light or flashlight handy. Whenever you have a dream, write whatever details you can remember. Or sketch an image from the dream. As time passes, you may detect some hidden messages or recurring themes.

- Collages are a great medium for dream work. Create a collage that includes colors, images, and/or words from your recurring dream.

- Create a diorama with images from your recurring dream in it.

This piece of artwork was created from a recycled framed canvas (the canvas is on the other side and not seen in this photo). The frame is what creates the mini-boxes. The theme in this piece is a recurring dream of a haunted house—the female spirit hangs from an eye hook.

My Happy Place

◆ ◆ ◆ ◆ ◆ ◆ ◆ ◆ ◆ ◆ ◆ ◆ ◆ ◆ ◆ ◆ ◆ ◆ ◆ ◆

Do you ever joke about "going to your Happy Place?" In this activity you can create one! Think about places, real or imagined, where you feel happy and relaxed. Or visualize what kind of place would bring a true sense of peace and calm for you.

The next step is to re-create it. There are many possibilities for going about this activity:

- Paint, draw, or sketch a picture of your Happy Place.

- If a photograph exists of the place already, frame it or include it in a piece of artwork.

- Using the same techniques in the Mini Shrines section (p.35), create a mini shrine of your Happy Place.

- If it's easier for you to describe it in written word, write a journal entry about your Happy Place and how it looks, feels, and smells to you.

Display your Happy Place creation somewhere you can see or access it when you are having a troublesome day. Visualize yourself in this calm place and take a five-minute mental vacation there.

Two Happy Places—the mountains and the beach are represented within altered tins.

Shadowboxing

♦ ♦ ♦ ♦ ♦ ♦ ♦ ♦ ♦ ♦ ♦ ♦ ♦ ♦ ♦ ♦ ♦ ♦

Sometimes, as young teenagers transition out of "little kid" interests to young adult interests, it can be bittersweet to leave behind toys, collections, or special items that had meaning to you as a child. Shadowbox collections can be a way to keep those special items around but in a contained and artistic manner that fits better into the ambiance of a teen's room.

Some examples of collections might be:

- small toy figurines
- rocks
- candy dispensers
- bottle caps
- iems found in nature
- shells
- gumball machine trinkets.

Shadowboxes are wooden frames filled with compartments for displaying items. Visit a craft shop, flea market, or wood shop where shadowboxes are commonly found. You may need to clean the shadowbox first if you are buying it second hand. If the shadowbox is brand new, you may want to sand it and paint it.

Arrange your collection items inside your shadowbox. Sometimes you will have extra collection pieces and not enough room for them. This is okay—you can rotate and rearrange the items in your shadowbox as often as you like. This keeps it interesting. If you find you have more space and not enough collection items this is also okay. You can leave spaces blank or you can create your own items to fill the empty spaces. For example, you can create a title for your collection and place it in one of the boxes. A title can be written on a piece of folded cardstock so that it has dimension and can stand on its own in the box. You can also be patient and add to the boxes as you add to your collection.

A collection of car-related toys from childhood displayed in a shadowbox.

Put Your Stamp on It

♦ ♦ ♦ ♦ ♦ ♦ ♦ ♦ ♦ ♦ ♦ ♦ ♦ ♦ ♦ ♦ ♦ ♦ ♦ ♦

Create a unique stamp that is truly your own. Stamps can be designed from a simple picture you have drawn; it can be a design or logo that symbolizes who you are; it can be your initials; or it can be a picture of something that metaphorically represents you. Your stamps can be used a few ways:

- If you send any thank-you cards or written letters, you can stamp the front of the envelope with it.

- You can create your own gift tags and mark them with your stamps.

- Stamp your books in place of a book plate.

- Take your stamp letterboxing! Letterboxing is a fun outdoor activity where having your own personal stamp is required. Letterboxing is an activity where you follow clues to find hidden boxes along hiking trails and landmarks. Inside these letterboxes are guest books where you leave your stamp's signature, so to speak. You also get to collect a stamp from the letterbox and add it to your own book of collected stamps. Letterboxing is especially fun for people who love getting outdoors, solving puzzles, orienteering, and exploring new places. For more information about letterboxing in the United States you can visit www.letterboxing.org. If you live outside of the United States, run a search online about letterboxing resources in your area.

How to make your own stamps:

- Carve a simple stamp out of a medium- or large-sized eraser.

- Create a stamp from a piece of recycled Styrofoam. The best Styrofoam to use is the kind that food typically gets packaged with, such as meats and produce.
  - First, thoroughly wash and dry the Styrofoam.
  - Cut out a piece of the Styrofoam that is small enough to fit in an ink pad (there are small- to large-size ink pads, so the size of your stamp can fit accordingly).
  - Carve your design into the Styrofoam using a pencil.
  - Use E6000 or superglue to attach a handle to your stamp. The handle can be anything from a wooden spool, an acorn cap, a small piece of scrap wood; or any other object that you can hold easily in your fingers.

- Stamp kits are also sold at craft stores and online art supply shops.

- Last, you can always design your own stamp and pay for someone else to create it for you, typically at office supply shops. This is quite costly, but for some people this is a feasible option.

However you create your stamp, you will need an inking medium to use it.

- Ink pads—Ink pads are the most convenient method for stamping but can also be expensive. Ink pads can be bought at arts and crafts supply shops.

- Paint—If you decide to use paint with your stamps, it is best to use a paintbrush to apply paint lightly to your stamp. If you dip your stamp directly into the paint, it will most likely get gloppy and leave a mess.

- Markers—You can always color over your stamp with a marker and then apply the stamp to paper. This is perhaps the easiest and least expensive method to experiment with.

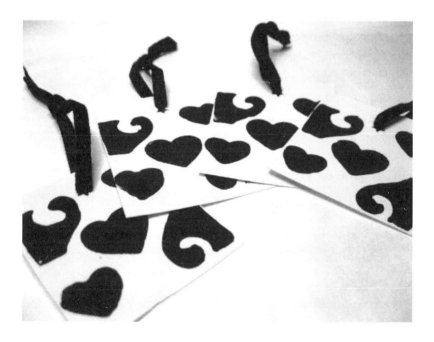

Gift tags created from a personal stamp.

Inspiration Decks

◆ ◆ ◆ ◆ ◆ ◆ ◆ ◆ ◆ ◆ ◆ ◆ ◆ ◆ ◆ ◆ ◆ ◆ ◆ ◆

Create your own deck of inspiration cards. Inspiration cards can be any size and any theme, as long as they provide inspiration for you. A quick and easy medium for making your own cards is to purchase blank Artist Trading Cards (found at art supply stores) or blank index cards (found at office supply stores). Cards can be decorated and used as tools for times when you need a boost of wisdom, a kind word, or a creative nudge. The cards can be kept in a special place for easy access and quick inspiration.

Inspiration Decks can contain almost any number of cards, but 10–20 seems to work best.

Inspiration Deck themes:

- Wisdom Deck—Create a deck of cards full of quotes and words of wisdom. The quotes can be from famous people, family members, friends, artists, or music lyrics.

- Power Deck—Create a deck of cards that encourage you to face your everyday life and its challenges. These cards can contain mantras (see section on Personal Mantras, p.46), affirmations, or reminders about who you are or your personal strengths.

- Creativity Deck—Create a deck of cards that encourages creativity:

  ◦ Story starters: e.g. "Grandmother walked into the kitchen and was knee deep in feathers..."

- o Creative writing challenges: e.g. "Write the story of Rapunzel told from the Hair's perspective."

- o Creative art challenges: e.g. "Create a sculpture using only recycled watch pieces."

- o General creativity: e.g. "Design a dress out of envelopes."

Once your deck is complete, where will you put it? You can make an Inspiration Jar to hold your cards, if the cards are really small. You can place the cards in a special bowl (see Letter to Your Child Self section, p.42, for directions on making a paper mache bowl), or you can even attach all of the cards to a key ring and bring them with you—cards on a key ring fit nicely in backpacks and lockers.

Inspiration Cards also make wonderful gifts for friends and loved ones!

A sample of cards from an Inspiration Deck.

Super Easy Accessories

♦ ♦ ♦ ♦ ♦ ♦ ♦ ♦ ♦ ♦ ♦ ♦ ♦ ♦ ♦ ♦ ♦ ♦ ♦ ♦

Accessories can be a fun way to express yourself and your individuality. Pendants, rings, pins, and hair accessories can all be created using these simple tools:

- Shrink plastic (the kind you bake to shrink—This can be found at craft stores or bought online). This plastic can be used to make pendants or pictures to go on a ring, necklace, headband, bobby pin, or brooch.

    - Illustrate a picture using permanent marker and/or colored pencils on the shrink plastic. Keep in mind your picture will shrink significantly, so make the original about two or three times bigger than the size you need. If you are making a ring, pin, or hair accessory, simply cut out the picture and it's ready to bake. If you are making a pendant for a necklace, cut out the picture and punch a hole in the top of it.

    - Bake your items according to directions on the package.

- E6000 glue.

- Jump rings (these are metal circles that will attach to your pendants if you are making them).

- Teeny tiny toys, knick knacks, beads, baubles, and buttons for decorating.

- Accessories (these can be purchased at any craft shop that sells jewelry supplies):
    - blank adjustable rings
    - plain bobby pins, metal barrettes, or headbands
    - ball chains for necklaces
    - blank pin backs.

Rings, hair accessories, and pins—To make your own rings, hair accessories, and pins, simply attach any of your small items to your accessory using the E6000 glue. Allow the item to dry per package instructions (usually 72 hours) before using.

Necklaces—Attach a jump ring to the pendant and it's ready to put on a ball chain necklace.

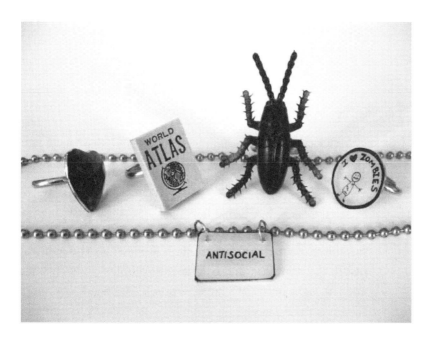

A sampling of rings along with a ball chain necklace.

Triptychs

◆ ◆ ◆ ◆ ◆ ◆ ◆ ◆ ◆ ◆ ◆ ◆ ◆ ◆ ◆ ◆ ◆ ◆

Triptychs are pieces of artwork created from three panels—the panels are usually connected via folds or hinges. The panels can be made of cardboard, wood, or other material. Blank triptychs can sometimes be purchased at craft shops. However, you can easily make your own by following these instructions:

- Cut out three panels from cardboard or foam board. You can make the panels equal size and shape or you can experiment with your own designs. Many triptychs have a center panel that is taller or a different shape than the exterior panels.

- Line up your panels, making sure the bottom is even (otherwise it won't stand correctly).

- You can connect your panels using string. However, you are going to need to make holes first for the string to go through.

- Use a pencil to mark two holes on each side of the panels where it touches another panel. The left exterior panel will have two holes where it connects to the central panel; the central panel will have two holes on each side; and the right panel will have two holes where it connects to the central panel.

Before you connect any panels, you will need to complete them. Decide on a theme for your triptych. Here are some ideas:

- Create a triptych that represents you in the past, present, and future.

- Write a poem or short story on your triptych.

- Create a self-portrait in the center panel. Use the side panels for quotes, poetry, pictures, collage, or paintings that express who you are.

- The triptych can be used as a tribute to someone you admire or someone that has passed away. Place a photo or draw a picture of the person in the center panel. Then decorate the end panels with memories about the person or what you admire about them.

When the panels are dry, you can simply tie string or use wire to connect your panels.

This triptych was created using recycled corrugated cardboard that was folded into three panels and cut into shape. Cardboard strips were glued on to create "frames" in the panel's centers. The triptych was them painted and decorated.

Paper Chains

♦ ♦

Paper chains may seem like a craft from your younger years, but in this activity you put a spin on it to make it teen-friendly.

First, let's review the basics of paper chains in case you've forgotten how to make them:

- You will need several strips of paper and a stapler. Your paper strips will need to be thin enough to create shape, but wide enough to create strength. This can take some experimenting, so play around with it.

- Create your initial starting link by stapling two ends of a paper strip together.

- To create the next link, slide a paper strip through the link, and then join the two ends together. Staple into place.

- Continue creating links to your chain until the chain is complete—this will depend on how long you want or need the chain to be.

Next, decide how you will use your paper chain (this will determine whether you can jump right in to make your chain all at once or if it'll be an ongoing activity). Here are some creative suggestions for Paper Chain projects:

- Create a Paper Chain Journal: Each day, choose a strip of paper and write about your day on it. Date it and add it to your chain.

- Write quotes or favorite music lyrics on the chain links.

- Create a Paper Chain simply for decoration. Choose paper that has wild, bold, and crazy patterns on it. If anyone in your home does scrapbooking, they may have some fun patterned paper they are not using and are willing to share. Use the chain to decorate your room— it can embellish doorways, windows, or decorate the perimeter of your bedroom.

- Create a Paper Chain with your friends:

  - If you have a friend who is ill or has moved, have each person write a message on a link and then create a chain for them. They can decorate their room with it and be reminded of your friendship.

  - Create a friendship Paper Chain. Invite your friends over and have a bunch of paper strips available. Have each friend write what they like about each person that is present. Then, each of your friends can create their own Paper Chain out of the links people wrote about them.

  - Create a Memory Chain—If someone you cared about has passed away, you and your friends can create a paper chain as a tribute to their memory. Each person simply writes about a memory they have of the person that has passed, or writes a comment such as "I'll miss you." The chain can be displayed where others can add to it or read it.

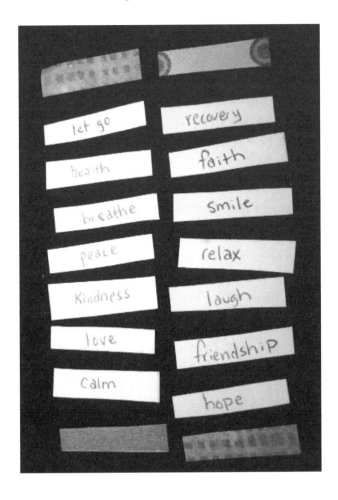

Strips of paper for a Paper Chain prior to being linked.

Art in Unexpected Places

◆ ◆ ◆ ◆ ◆ ◆ ◆ ◆ ◆ ◆ ◆ ◆ ◆ ◆ ◆ ◆ ◆

Many times we find art in unexpected places that is either illegal (graffiti), profane (bathroom stall walls), or detrimental to the environment (names and initials carved into trees). Personally, I love the idea of leaving your artwork, or "mark" so to speak, in unexpected places, but people can lose sight of creative ways to this without harm. It is possible, however.

Creating Art in Unexpected Places can be a fun diversion from everyday reality. It uses your creativity and ingenuity, and even encourages you to explore the world a little more. Look at these examples of Art in Unexpected Places to see what I mean:

- Create miniature cards that have positive messages written in them, e.g. "Find beauty in this day" or "You are cared about." Disperse your cards in places people will find them, such as a friend's car seat; a friend's locker; a library book; a waiting room table; in a café, etc… Do not sign them or leave your name. Part of the fun of these exercises is the mystery.

- Do you do a lot of walking or hiking? Find a creative way to leave your "mark" made completely out of natural items. For example, leave acorn caps lined on tree limbs; arrange rocks in a certain pattern; weave a clump of grasses along a trail (leave them rooted); or use natural materials to create art outdoors and leave it for someone to find. Fairy houses and cairns are perfect examples of beautiful artwork people leave behind that says "Someone has been here." If you have ever come across such art in the woods, mountains, or along a trail, you understand the mysterious feeling it evokes.

- If you live in an urban or city environment, you can create similar artwork but you may have to be more creative. You can always collect natural items from a city park and use these materials later when needed. Imagine coming across a beautiful pattern of rocks near a fire hydrant or leaves creating a winding path along the sidewalk.

- Create art that inspires others to play along with you. For example, the next time you are at a café, leave a mini piece of your artwork (e.g. a drawing or an Artist Trading Card you created) in a newspaper or on a table. Tag the artwork with a message: "This piece of artwork has been created in the hope it will inspire others to leave Art in Unexpected Places as well. Carry on the tradition and make some shareable art of your own."

- Create decorated bookmarks or notes and leave them in library books. Here is a nice example: Leave a beautifully illustrated note in a book about beauty or self-esteem that says, "You are beautiful." What do you think the reaction will be of the person who finds it?

However you choose to create and leave your artwork, I do have some reminders:

- Make sure you are not littering or causing other harm by leaving your artwork where it is.

- Do not use envelopes as this makes people highly suspicious.

- Keep it positive and upbeat.

You can help make the world more beautiful with your creativity.

A heart made from acorn caps.

Tribute to a Special Memory

◆ ◆ ◆ ◆ ◆ ◆ ◆ ◆ ◆ ◆ ◆ ◆ ◆ ◆ ◆ ◆ ◆ ◆

Many times we go on special trips or partake in an event and end up with mementos and memorabilia. Some people throw these items away, others save them for scrapbooking or store them away for a rainy day. For this project, choose a day, memory, or event that had special meaning to you. If you have any items from that day or span of time, gather them together. You can even draw your own pictures, write anecdotes about it, or re-create some of the items that might have been part of the experience, such as movie stubs or concert tickets. The event can be as grand as a vacation, or as simple as Chinese take-out with a friend. Whichever moment you choose, it's yours to honor it.

A tribute to fond memories of art camp.

Choose a format for displaying all of these items. There are several mediums to choose from: Collage; shadowbox; scrapbook; altered book; or a triptych. You can even purchase framed boxes at photo and craft stores if you want to display your items in this format.

PART II

Journaling

◇◇◇◇◇◇◇◇◇◇◇◇◇◇◇◇

If you love to write and/or draw, journaling is a creative way to release some pent-up creative energy. When picking out a journal, a sketchbook-sized journal with blank pages is best for a variety of journaling projects—drawing, sketching, doodling, writing, and even collages.

However, many teens complain about not knowing what to draw, write, or put in their journals. Here are some journaling ideas to get your creative juices flowing:

- Cut out pictures and words from magazines and glue them to your journal pages for inspiration.

- Glue envelopes onto random journal pages—glue the flat side to the page. Next time you get a good grade on a paper or a fun note from a friend in school, fold it up and tuck it inside the envelope.

- Glue or tape mementos into your journal—photos, ticket stubs from an event or movie, bubble gum wrappers, notes or quotes from friends, etc…

- Make some lists:
  - the most mysterious and/or magical moments of your life
  - your favorite movies
  - your favorite books
  - things that have made you laugh
  - what you love about spring, summer, winter, and/or autumn
  - if you had a magic wand
  - if you had extra money
  - how you want to celebrate your next birthday
  - five things you want to accomplish before you turn 21.

- Draw or sketch a floor plan for how you want your future house, apartment, or flat to be.

- Write down favorite song lyrics that have meaning to you.

- Doodle. You can also save doodles from your school note-books—cut out your favorite doodles and glue them into your journal.

- If you can think of nothing to write or draw, simply decorate the borders of your journal pages—later on when you do feel inspired to write in your journal, you'll have beautiful pages to write on.

Autobiography in Metaphors

♦ ♦

Write a paragraph or two describing who you are using only metaphors. Metaphors are a figure of speech—they are used when a person wants to express that something is of the same likeness or situation as something else. Here are some examples of metaphors:

- It's raining cats and dogs outside.

- My legs have turned to rubber.

- The teacher barked at me for not doing my homework.

To get you started, answer these questions:

- Are you a sunrise or a sunset?

- If you were a shape, what shape would you be?

- What color crayon are you?

- If you were a breakfast cereal, which cereal would you be?

- If you were a famous landmark, which one would you be?

- Which type of tree are you?

- What type of candy are you?

- If you were an animal, which animal would you be?

- If you were a body of water, what type of water would you be?

- If you were a mythical creature, which one would you be?

- Are you Earth, Air, Water, or Fire?

- Which fairy tale character are you?

- Which season are you?

- What famous piece of artwork are you?

- If you were an item from the beach, what would you be?

- If you were an item from the forest, what would you be?

- Are you North, East, South, or West?

- What famous novel or book are you?

You've got the hang of it now, right? Continue to create more metaphors if you like.

The next step is to take your metaphors and "stretch" them. To stretch your metaphors, add more detail to them. For example, pretend you said you are a river in response to "Which body of water are you?"

- Are you a fast-flowing river or a slow-moving river?

- Is your water cool or warm?

- Is your river clean and full of life, or polluted and in need of care?

- Has anything especially wonderful or tragic happened in your river?

- When is the river calm?

- What causes ripples or waves in the water?

Stretch your metaphors as much as you can in order to bring out who you are or how you might describe yourself. When they are all completed, pick out your favorite metaphors you wrote and combine them to create your autobiography.

A Kaleidoscope of Friends

◆ ◆ ◆ ◆ ◆ ◆ ◆ ◆ ◆ ◆ ◆ ◆ ◆ ◆ ◆ ◆ ◆ ◆ ◆ ◆

Friends are a reflection of who we are. Rarely do we find one friend who meets every one of our needs for friendship or understands each and every aspect of ourselves. There is a reason for each and every friendship you have, and each of these friendships ultimately brings out a part, or parts, of you that may differ from one friend to the next.

Create a list of your current friends. Write down some responses to the following (do this for each friend on your list):

- When you are with this friend, what parts of your personality stand out? For example, are you more social? Quiet? Silly? Reserved?

- What keeps you in this friendship?

- What do you bring to the relationship? What does your friend bring to the relationship?

- What are your favorite things about this friend?

- How do you think this friend would describe you?

You can take this exercise and challenge yourself further by seeing if you can represent your kaleidoscope of friends visually. Can you create a piece of art that shows what your kaleidoscope of friends might look like?

Snapshot Moments

◆ ◆ ◆ ◆ ◆ ◆ ◆ ◆ ◆ ◆ ◆ ◆ ◆ ◆ ◆ ◆ ◆ ◆ ◆

Think back to a pleasant moment in your life and try to pull out a split second of that moment—What was going on around you? Who were you with? Were you inside or outside? Was there a certain sensory experience attached to this split second, e.g. the sound of a wave, or the smell of a barbecue, or the taste of something yummy?

In this journal exercise, choose some split second moments to write about. The challenge, however, is to try and break down the split second to a true snapshot picture. Try and describe the moment in as few words as possible.

Some examples:

- a warm cup of coffee in my hands; steam rising in the brisk fall morning air

- toes buried in warm sand; bathing suit wet; feeling serene

- full moon rising; dark sky; first kiss.

Part of the fun of this activity is the mystery—if anyone else were to read your snapshot moment, they will most likely have no idea what moment you are writing about unless they were there with you, or you told them specifically. Snapshot moments take on a life of their own—they are magical like that.

Comic Life

◆ ◆ ◆ ◆ ◆ ◆ ◆ ◆ ◆ ◆ ◆ ◆ ◆ ◆ ◆ ◆ ◆ ◆ ◆

It's good to laugh at yourself now and then. We all make mistakes, we all do stupid things, and let's face it—humans are not perfect. These moments were made for comic strips!

Draw a humorous comic strip of yourself. Try one of these suggestions or make up your own:

- Create a comic strip of a time you did something clumsy and/or completely embarrassed yourself.

- Create a comic about a time you over-reacted in a situation.

- Create a comic strip about how you react when faced with a situation or thing you fear.

- Draw a comic of how you react when the "spotlight" is on you, e.g. when people sing Happy Birthday to you.

- Draw a comic strip of yourself in a grumpy mood.

Mini Graphic Novels

◆ ◆ ◆ ◆ ◆ ◆ ◆ ◆ ◆ ◆ ◆ ◆ ◆ ◆ ◆ ◆ ◆ ◆ ◆

Similar to Comic Life, create these comic strips or Mini Graphic Novels based on the ideas and titles below. Experiment with different sized boxes and spacing for your pictures, words, and speech bubbles.

- I took the blame for it…
- I looked at your text messages…
- I hate you…
- I love you…
- OMG!
- I wish…
- I have a secret…
- What you do not know is…
- I pretend…
- Backstabber
- I hate being perfect
- I wish I were _____
- Revenge!
- What goes on in the bathroom at school…
- What happens on the school bus…
- I know something you don't know…

- I'm grounded because _____

- I saw it on the internet…

- My teacher doesn't know…

- That's not true!

- If her/his parents only knew…

- My counselor/My therapist

Wishes

◆ ◆ ◆ ◆ ◆ ◆ ◆ ◆ ◆ ◆ ◆ ◆ ◆ ◆ ◆ ◆ ◆ ◆ ◆

Fill up some blank pages in your journal with wishes and hedonistic musings.

Creative suggestions:

- If you have some favorite clothing catalogues, cut out favorite items and paste them in your journal. Pretend it is a shopping spree and you can have whatever clothing and accessories you desire. Fill up the page/s with clothing, shoes, and/or accessories you would love to own.

- If you enjoy traveling, include some travel itineraries. Pretend there are no obstacles—imagine you can go anywhere. Where would you go? What would you do each day on this amazing trip? Cut out pictures and photos from travel websites or travel brochures and paste them in with your itinerary.

- Pretend you have no time constraints—create a reading list of books you want to read.

- With the same idea in mind, create a list of all the movies you would love to see.

- Write a list of five accomplishments you want to achieve in your life.

- Write a list of 20 places you want to visit in your lifetime. What types of places get you interested in traveling this world? Consider the following: Places that let you see wildlife up close; roadside attractions; famous eateries; tropical islands; haunted establishments; ghost towns; amusement parks; adventure travel; spiritual places; or secluded areas. There are many destinations to choose from!

The Ultimate Day

♦ ♦ ♦ ♦ ♦ ♦ ♦ ♦ ♦ ♦ ♦ ♦ ♦ ♦ ♦ ♦ ♦ ♦ ♦

Now and then you may have a day off of school or work and then be left wondering, "What should I do today?" But, if you are like many people, by the time you have gone through the motions of your morning, somehow the day has slipped by and you are left kicking yourself that you didn't use the time off more wisely.

The Ultimate Day is a journaling exercise where you plan ahead for a day off—not just any day off, but a relaxing or self-indulgent day off.

Start with an entire day. If your school was canceled for the day, what would be a great way to spend the day?

Things to consider:

- How late or how early do you wake up?

- What will you eat for your meals?

- What activities will you do during the day? Will you stay home or will you venture out?

- Are you alone or will you share this day (or part of it) with someone else?

- What is the goal of the day—is it to relax? Have fun? Socialize?

You can also write about smaller increments of time. For example, what would the Ultimate Morning look like? Or list several ways to make the most of 10 minutes. The next time you have an unplanned block of time you can refer to this journal entry for inspiration.

Freedom From

Freedom From explores who you are and how you would live your life if there were zero roadblocks. It's an activity to look at the core of who you are and your desires. We all have obstacles that keep us from living up to our full potential or living out every aspect of life the way we would like.

In this writing activity, pretend you have freedom from *all* obstacles. Pretend you wake up tomorrow and life is exactly how you want it to be—what does it look like?

Things to consider:

- Do you live alone or with other people? If you live with other people, what are their personalities like and how do they act around you?

- Where do you live—near the ocean? In the city? In the mountains?

- When you walk into your home, how does it feel? How does your home look? Does your home smell like anything, e.g. fresh baked cookies or flowers?

- What does the yard look and smell like? For example, do you have gardens or landscaping? Do you even have a yard?

- Do you work? If so, what is your job?

- What do you do for hobbies?

- Do you have pets?

- Do you travel?

- What kind of friends do you have?

- What do you and your friends do for fun?

- What do you like to do in the evening?

- What do you use for transportation?

Rites of Passage Plan

◆ ◆ ◆ ◆ ◆ ◆ ◆ ◆ ◆ ◆ ◆ ◆ ◆ ◆ ◆ ◆ ◆ ◆ ◆ ◆

Rites of passage visit us at many ages and stages of life. We learn to walk, talk, go to school, graduate from school, find a romantic partner, commit, split up, have children, buy that first car or first home, etc. Sometimes, if you do not plan ahead for these rites of passage, they slip by unnoticed, or take us by surprise, unprepared.

Celebratory Rites of Passage

Create a plan for how you can recognize yourself and your accomplishments when they do happen. This plan can include anything from treating yourself to something special, a moment of quiet contemplation, visiting a place that holds meaning to you, lighting a candle, or a gathering of loved ones to celebrate with you. Write this plan down in your journal so you can refer to it.

Challenging Rites of Passage

Tough moments are going to happen—it's a fact of life. And nothing feels worse than being taken by surprise when the news is not good. Create a "Back Up Plan." Plan ahead for how you'll manage a difficult rite of passage. Even though it may feel uncomfortable creating such a plan, if you ever end up needing it you may be grateful to have it to fall back on.

- What are your passions and/or hobbies? If things become challenging what can you channel your energy into?

- What foods are energizing and healing for you? What are some of your favorite comfort foods?

- What physical activity do you enjoy doing? As you probably know, exercise and activity can help to reduce stress.

- What movies cheer you up or give you balance?

- What are some moments that have melted your heart, made you laugh, and/or appreciated life? Write them down so you can remember them when life gets hard.

- Who will be there for you when you need the support? Consider friends, family, teachers, counselors, mentors, church or community members, etc…

Hilarious Haikus

♦ ♦ ♦ ♦ ♦ ♦ ♦ ♦ ♦ ♦ ♦ ♦ ♦ ♦ ♦ ♦ ♦ ♦

Many of us have learned to write traditional haikus in school. Haikus are poems of three lines. The first line is five syllables; the second line is seven syllables; and the last line is five syllables. Traditionally haikus were written about nature and beauty. However, my favorite use of haikus is to be a bit snarky, dark humored or to challenge my friends in thematic haikus—we come up with a theme and see who can write the most clever haiku about it. There is something ironic and humorous about seeing haikus dress up in this new language.

At first this may sound foolish—how can haikus be *funny*? The best way may be to try it. Challenge your friends or try one for yourself:

- Write a haiku about a clique in your school.

- Write a haiku about your homework assignment.

- Write a haiku about something you'd find on the school lunch menu.

- Write a haiku about your principal.

- Write a haiku about Monday mornings.

- Write a haiku about a sibling.

- Write a haiku about a bad habit of yours.

Venting in Gibberish

♦ ♦ ♦ ♦ ♦ ♦ ♦ ♦ ♦ ♦ ♦ ♦ ♦ ♦ ♦ ♦ ♦ ♦ ♦ ♦

Write a journal entry where you are venting about something—but write about it in a humorous style:

- Make funny rhymes.
- When you can't find a rhyming word, make one up.
- Create other new words or phrases.
- Exaggerate the details.
- Write it in completely made up language.
- Write it backwards or in spirals.
- Use alliteration—repeat certain sounds or use words that start mostly with the letter ____.

If you're feeling even more creative, illustrate some pictures to go along with it.

PART III

Miniature Projects for Personal Spaces

◇◇◇◇◇◇◇◇◇◇◇◇◇◇◇◇◇◇◇◇◇◇◇◇◇◇◇◇◇◇◇◇◇◇◇◇◇

Bedrooms and school lockers are the perfect canvas for self-expression. There are books and web pages on designing bedrooms for today's youths, so I am not going to re-create the wheel by addressing *major* changes to your room. I will, however, provide some creative ideas for smaller projects you can create for your room and locker (or other personal spaces like a car) to personalize them.

Bedroom Pop Art

♦ ♦ ♦ ♦ ♦ ♦ ♦ ♦ ♦ ♦ ♦ ♦ ♦ ♦ ♦ ♦ ♦ ♦ ♦

Modern recycled goods can be creatively displayed and hung in your bedroom. For example, if you have a favorite junky breakfast cereal you can hang a clean, empty box of it on your wall. Or, create a themed piece of art repeating such cereal boxes on your wall, e.g. around a door frame. See what other uses of recycled goods you can create in your room using Pop Art themes.

Wooden Drawer Pulls

◆ ◆ ◆ ◆ ◆ ◆ ◆ ◆ ◆ ◆ ◆ ◆ ◆ ◆ ◆ ◆ ◆ ◆ ◆

Do you have any wooden furniture in your room that has drawer pulls/knobs? If so, you can most likely personalize them:

- Check and make sure the knobs are made of wood (and not veneer/artificial wood).

- Can you remove the knobs? If they are attached only with screws, you should be able to detach the knobs. If they have been glued in you will not be able to do this activity.

- Ask your parent/guardian if it is okay to paint these knobs.

If they say it's okay, choose acrylic paints to design your own drawer knobs! Remember to allow the knobs to dry before screwing them back into place.

Light Switch Covers

◆ ◆ ◆ ◆ ◆ ◆ ◆ ◆ ◆ ◆ ◆ ◆ ◆ ◆ ◆ ◆ ◆ ◆ ◆

Light switch covers are inexpensive and easy to alter.

- Ask a parent/guardian's permission to replace the light switch plates in your room.

- If they say it's okay, go ahead and ask them to remove the light switch plates from your room and give them to you.

  - Decorate the switch plates with permanent markers using a design, picture, or pattern that fits your room or style.

  - Ask your parent/guardian to put them back on the light switches.

  - If you mess up or do not like what you created, these covers can be found at hardware stores and are inexpensive to replace.

Mini Memo Boards
and Corkboards

♦ ♦ ♦ ♦ ♦ ♦ ♦ ♦ ♦ ♦ ♦ ♦ ♦ ♦ ♦ ♦ ♦ ♦ ♦ ♦

It can be helpful to have a small space in your locker where you can hang important reminders and messages. A small-sized corkboard works best and can be purchased at an office store. You can also create your own memo board if you need—just find a thick piece of cardboard and cut a rectangle or other simple shape out of it. Cover this cardboard completely in decorative paper (e.g. wrap it like a present) and secure it with glue or tape.

Altered Pushpins and Thumbtacks

◆ ◆ ◆ ◆ ◆ ◆ ◆ ◆ ◆ ◆ ◆ ◆ ◆ ◆ ◆ ◆ ◆ ◆ ◆

- You will need E6000 glue, thumbtacks and small trinkets, novelties, and/or fun small objects. Buttons, baubles, cabochons, gumball machine prizes, googly eyes, game pieces, etc...can all be used to make fun thumbtacks to use on your memo board.

- Follow the safety guidelines per your glue bottle—make sure you have plenty of fresh air while using glue.

- Apply a small amount of glue to the flat top of the thumbtack and then place one of your novelty items on top of it. Allow thumbtack to dry for 72 hours before using.

Altered Clothespins
and Hang Line

◆ ◆ ◆ ◆ ◆ ◆ ◆ ◆ ◆ ◆ ◆ ◆ ◆ ◆ ◆ ◆ ◆ ◆ ◆

- Purchase traditional clothespins.

- Glue strips of decorative paper and/or words from a magazine onto the clothespins. Allow the clothespins to dry.

- Cut a ribbon to the size of your memo board. Use two of your altered thumbtacks to hold it in place. Attach the clothespins to the ribbon like a clothesline. Now you can attach mini messages and reminders to yourself here.

Magnets

♦ ♦ ♦ ♦ ♦ ♦ ♦ ♦ ♦ ♦ ♦ ♦ ♦ ♦ ♦ ♦ ♦ ♦

- Purchase magnets from a craft or hardware store. The smallest round size is best.

- Do the same thing you did with the thumbtacks and use E6000 glue to attach fun items to the magnets. Allow these to dry for 72 hours before using.

- Use these magnets inside your locker to attach reminders and messages to yourself.

Key Chains

♦ ♦

- You will need shrink plastic; jump rings (one per each keychain you plan to create); and key chains for this project.

- Read and follow the directions that come with your shrink plastic. (Shrink plastic can be ordered online at many craft sites.)

- Draw a design or picture onto the shrink plastic—the picture will shrink when you put it in the oven so make sure you draw the picture about three times bigger than the actual size you want it to be.

- Cut out your picture and punch a hole through the top of it using a hole punch.

- Per instructions that came with your plastic, bake the plastic as directed.

- Allow the plastic to cool.

- Attach a small jump ring to your picture and then attach the picture to a key ring.

Altered Tin Containers

♦ ♦ ♦ ♦ ♦ ♦ ♦ ♦ ♦ ♦ ♦ ♦ ♦ ♦ ♦ ♦ ♦ ♦ ♦

If you have a locker at school, work, or the gym, small tin containers can be useful for storing teeny tiny items. Hair elastics, elastics for orthodontic work, small erasers, and even mints/candy (if you are allowed to have it in your locker) can be easily stored and stacked in your locker. Miniature tins used for candles, mints, or lip gloss can be washed and re-used for this project.

- Make sure the tin is thoroughly cleaned and dried.

- Lightly sand any areas where you will want to apply glue or paint.

- Decorate the lid or outside of the tin with decorative papers, acrylic paints, or ribbon.

- Allow tin to dry…and it's ready to use!

Mini Flag Banners

◆ ◆

Mini banners can be made for your bedroom or your locker.

- Measure how long a banner you will need for the space you want and then add an extra foot (to allow enough room for tying or hanging).

- Cut out multiple rectangles or diamonds out of paper—when folded in half, rectangles will create square-shaped flags. Diamonds will create triangle flags. Also, consider whether you want the flags to be the same size or not. The size of the flag is going to depend on the space you are using and how big or small you want the flags to be. Some people prefer their flags to be all the same size and shape—others will want to mix it up and create more variety. It's up to you.

- If you want to decorate the flags, do so before attaching them to the string. Flags can be stamped, colored, or trimmed with special scissors for a decorative effect.

- Now apply a small amount of glue to one half of the flag, and where the fold line is. Lay your string across the fold line. Now fold the flag over and glue into place. Repeat this for each flag, leaving space between flags as you go.

- Allow the flags to dry and then hang them up.

Moustache Pencil Toppers

◆ ◆ ◆ ◆ ◆ ◆ ◆ ◆ ◆ ◆ ◆ ◆ ◆ ◆ ◆ ◆ ◆ ◆ ◆ ◆

If you're a teenager, photo props are a must have. You never know when a friend is going to walk past with his or her camera, and it's best to be prepared. Moustaches are a goofy prop to have on hand for group photos with your friends or those moments when you've had too much sugar at lunch or your best friend needs a laugh.

- You will need a pencil, tape, or glue, and one of the moustache mediums listed below.

- There are several ways to create moustaches:

    o Sew a plush moustache using felt and cotton stuffing.

    o Cut a moustache out of poster board or cardstock.

    o Cut a moustache out of super-thin cork (cork comes in sheets at various office and craft shops).

    o My favorite moustache medium is actually wooden angel wings—the "wings" look more like moustaches to me (see photo).

- Next, apply the moustache to the top end of your pencil. Depending on what you used for a medium, you may need to glue the moustache to the pencil (and allow it to dry overnight) or you can tape it. If possible, make a bunch of these and keep them stored in your locker.

PART IV

Incorporating the Activities into Treatment—A Section for Counselors

◇◇

If you are a counselor billing an outside source for your services, you may be familiar with treatment goals and objectives. I have highlighted some treatment areas in this final section. Each treatment area contains sample goals you might find on a treatment plan as well as activities found in this book that can meet the goal partially or fully. The activities are meant to provide some creative tools and ideas for ways to engage teens in therapy and self-expression. As with any intervention, use your professional judgment to decipher if these activities are truly appropriate and relevant for your clients.

Developing a Therapeutic Alliance with Your Client

◆ ◆ ◆ ◆ ◆ ◆ ◆ ◆ ◆ ◆ ◆ ◆ ◆ ◆ ◆ ◆ ◆ ◆ ◆

GOAL: The client and clinician will establish a therapeutic relationship (during those first initial sessions).

- Mixed Media Self-Portraits (p.50)—Ask the client to create a self-portrait using simple mixed materials you have in your office already, e.g. newsprint, recycled paper, colored paper, markers, crayons, glue, etc. A self-portrait can be a gentle way for the client to start expressing him/herself in therapy.

- Many of the activities from Part III (Miniature Projects for Personal Spaces) can be used to work on developing a trusting and therapeutic alliance with the client. These activities are fun, interactive, and encourage self-expression without delving into clinical issues. In addition, many teens are more likely to engage in a conversation if there is an activity on hand (this takes the pressure off feeling obligated to talk or make eye contact).

Mood Disorders, Anxiety Disorders, and General Coping Skills

♦ ♦ ♦ ♦ ♦ ♦ ♦ ♦ ♦ ♦ ♦ ♦ ♦ ♦ ♦ ♦ ♦ ♦

GOAL: The client will practice at least three distress tolerance skills.

- Personal Mantras (p.46)—Have the client choose a phrase or word that she can focus on when feeling distress. Ask the client to include this mantra in a piece of artwork. If the client likes what she has created, she can display it somewhere she can see it often to remind her of her mantra.

- Visualization/imagery skills:

  - My Personal Totem (p.28)—Ask the client to create a totem of his spirit or guide animals that are helping him through this phase of life. The client can practice visualizing these animal guides around him when feeling distressed.

  - Mini Shrines (p.35)—Create a mini Zen garden with the client. Ask the client to choose a time before the next session to practice creating a design in the sand, or rearranging the rocks in the garden for calming.

  - My Happy Place (p.60)—Help the client define her Happy Place and then assign her to re-create it in a piece of artwork. She can use this as a "visual" to refer to when feeling distraught. Ask her to practice visualizing herself in her Happy Place at least once before the next session.

- Calming/relaxation skills:

  - Photojournalism (p.23)—If the client enjoys photography and has a camera, assign him to create a mini photojournal of details in his environment that he finds calming.

  - Mandalas (p.48)—Have the client draw or color a mandala when feeling distressed as a way to calm and re-focus the mind.

  - Journaling (p.81)—Assign 15 minutes of journaling a day as a way to release emotions and calm the mind.

- Distraction skills:

  - The Creative Hunting and Gathering activity (p.11) can be assigned as a distraction intervention.

  - Body Art (p.27)—The client can use washable tattoo markers at home to decorate her arms, feet, and legs (as long as the parents/guardians are okay with it). Henna designs and other intricate patterns can be very soothing for some clients—it can help them distract from worry thoughts, obsessions, and flight of ideas. Body art can also become a nice ritual to replace cutting and skin-picking behaviors.

  - Paper Chains (p.72) can be a calming distraction for some clients due to the repetitive motion of the activity. If this strategy works well, your client may need to get creative with multiple paper chain projects. He can create a paper chain of thank-yous for someone who has helped him out; he can make paper chain decorations for his hospital room, group home, bedroom, or your office; or challenge him to put a new spin on the paper chain design itself, e.g. can he make square links?

GOAL: The client will practice at least three new skills in mindfulness.

- Photojournalism (p.23)—If the client enjoys photography, ask her to photograph what catches her attention. Have her describe the details of the objects that made them appealing for photographing.

- Body Art (p.27)—The client can complete this activity assignment at home to practice mindfulness. Instruct the client to hone in on the sensation of the skin as he decorates it.

- Mini Shrines (p.35)—Have the client create a mini shrine that helps remind her to practice mindfulness. The shrine could be dedicated to a word or phrase such as "breathe in, breathe out" to help her focus on being in the body and taking in breath.

- Personal Mantras (p.46)—Have the client create a phrase or "power word" he can focus on when feeling distress.

- Mandalas (p.48)—Have the client color a mandala and take in the calming motion of coloring while quieting the mind.

- Snapshot Moments (p.86)—Ask the client to focus on the minute details of a pleasant memory to practice mindfulness. Have her write about it in her journal.

GOAL: The client will practice and use two new ways to express feelings safely.

- ACEOs (p.17)—Have the client create a series of ACEOs that evoke varying emotions, such as anger, sadness, bliss, jealousy, despair, loneliness, and fear.

- Photojournalism (p.23)—If the client enjoys photography, assign him to capture a feeling in a series of photos. For example, ask the client to photograph images that make him feel sadness or anger and put them together in a collage.

- Me, Myself, and I—Three Building Blocks (p.24)—The client can use the three blocks to represent three different emotions. Each side of the block can have an image, color, or word that reflects on that emotion.

- Emo Dolls (p.56)—You can have the client create Emo Dolls representing a variety of emotions. If the client likes the idea of this activity, have her choose from three to five emotions to make Emo Dolls of. You can also have the client create some Emo Dolls specific to a situation.

- My Happy Place (p.60)—Ask the client to create a mini version of his Happy Place and to explain what it is about this place (real or imagined) that makes him feel so happy there.

- Journaling (p.81)—Assign the client to 15 minutes of journaling a day to release pent-up emotions. Many of the Mini Graphic Novels' themes (p.88) encourage feelings expression.

Family Dynamics and Family Roles

♦ ♦ ♦ ♦ ♦ ♦ ♦ ♦ ♦ ♦ ♦ ♦ ♦ ♦ ♦ ♦ ♦ ♦ ♦

GOAL: The client will explore and define the roles within his/her own family.

- A Metaphorical Family Tree (p.30)—Ask the client to create a Metaphorical Family Tree. This Tree can provide a "visual" for both the client and clinician to refer to when discussing family issues and defining roles with the client's family. It is also a convenient tool for exploring family dynamics—for example, you might ask the client: "I notice you are a hidden branch on this tree. What does this branch need in order to grow taller and more in the open?"

- Themed Family Portraits (p.53)—Family portraits are another "visual" for clients and clinicians to refer to when discussing family roles and personalities.

Attention Deficit Disorders

♦ ♦ ♦ ♦ ♦ ♦ ♦ ♦ ♦ ♦ ♦ ♦ ♦ ♦ ♦ ♦ ♦ ♦ ♦

GOAL: The client will practice listening skills and following directions appropriately.

- Any multi-step activity in this book can be completed by client to practice following directions.

GOAL: The client will practice calming activities that help him/her slow down racing thoughts.

- Photojournalism (p.23)—Have the client photograph things that feel calming to him. Have him create a collection of these photos for display or easy access, such as in a photo album or framed on the wall.

- Body Art (p.27)—The client can use washable tattoo markers to create body art at home as a calming activity (only if the client finds it calming and the guardian/parent is okay with it).

- Personal Mantras (p.46)—Help the client figure out an appropriate mantra for calming and then assign her to create a piece of art around it. She can hang or display this piece of art where she can remind herself to practice it.

- Mandalas (p.48)—Ask your client to experiment with illustrating and/or coloring mandalas to see if he finds it calming.

- Paper Chains (p.72)—Again, the repetitive nature of this activity can be quite calming for some. Create a paper chain with your client to see if she finds it soothing.

GOAL: The client will practice organizational skills.

The client and clinician can work together creating fun organizational tools for the teen's locker or home.

- Mini Memo Boards and Corkboards (p.104)—A client can use memo or corkboards to keep track of test dates, appointments, or to attach gentle reminders about personal goals.

- Altered Pushpins and Thumbtacks (p.105)—Make these fun thumbtacks with your client—she is probably more likely to make use of her memo board with these engaging, attractive, and fun thumbtacks.

- Altered Clothespins and Hang Line (p.106)—If your client prefers the clothesline approach of keeping track of important dates and reminders, then help him create some altered clothespins and a hang line for his locker or room.

- Magnets (p.107)—This activity is too fun to pass up. Talk with your client about how she manages her time while making these magnets. When the magnets have dried, encourage your client to try them in her locker. She can attach reminders to her locker about upcoming appointments or other events she needs to keep track of.

- Altered Tin Containers (p.109)—If your client has a lot of small items that are getting lost at home or school (orthodontic elastics, for example), then create one or more altered tin containers to help him organize these items.

Disruptive Behavior Disorders and Oppositional Defiant Disorder

◆ ◆ ◆ ◆ ◆ ◆ ◆ ◆ ◆ ◆ ◆ ◆ ◆ ◆ ◆ ◆ ◆ ◆

GOAL: The client will participate in at least one pro-social activity or hobby a week.

- Artist Trading Cards (p.17)—If the client enjoys creating Artist Trading Cards, develop a way he can actually trade with other artists. Some communities have local gatherings and trade events. There are also online communities where he can get involved with other ATC participants.

- If the client enjoys doing artwork, then assign her to work on creative activity at least 15 minutes a day. If the client is able to follow through with this goal, incrementally increase the time she spends on it daily.

- Art in Unexpected Places (p.75)—Depending on your client, this may need to be a supervised activity. However, this section lists a few ways your client can get involved in creative pro-social activities.

GOAL: The client will assess whether his current behavior is leading him toward his life goals.

- Life Map (p.33)—Have the client create a Life Map that includes a compass rose. Ask him to define what North, East, South, and West represent to him. Which direction is the client heading at this point in his life?

- Rites of Passage Passport book (p.54)—Help your client create a Rites of Passage Passport book and then discuss what she'll need in order to accomplish these goals. Have her assess if she is heading in the right direction toward attaining these goals, or what she needs to do in order to be heading toward success.

- A Kaleidoscope of Friends (p.85)—This is a journaling activity but you can modify it to meet your client's need. Explore the friendships your client currently has and discuss how these friends help or hinder the client's success in making healthy and positive choices for a happier future.

Substance Use/Abuse

◆ ◆ ◆ ◆ ◆ ◆ ◆ ◆ ◆ ◆ ◆ ◆ ◆ ◆ ◆ ◆ ◆ ◆ ◆

GOAL: *The client will participate in at least one non-substance-related activity or hobby a week.*

- Artist Trading Cards (p.17)—If your client enjoys creating Artist Trading Cards, develop a way she can actually trade with other artists. Some communities have local gatherings and trade events. There are also online communities where she can get involved with other ATC participants.

- If the client enjoys doing artwork, assign him to work on an art project for a set period of time each day or week.

- Put Your Stamp on It (p.63)—If your client enjoys outdoor adventures, encourage her to try letterboxing. For more information on letterboxing, search the internet. There are online letterboxing sites which will differ from country to country.

- Art in Unexpected Places (p.75)—This section offers several ideas for non-substance-related activities.

- Journaling (p.81)—Have the client journal about his addiction, recovery, or sobriety.

GOAL: *The client will participate in substance abuse treatment.*

- Mini Shrine (p.35)—Some substance abuse treatment programs encourage their clients to lean on their spiritual and religious beliefs to help them through the recovery process. If the client has such beliefs have her create a

Mini Shrine dedicated to them. This Mini Shrine can be placed at home or in her locker where it can remind her of her efforts to overcome her difficulties.

GOAL: *The client will define how he/she wants to live his/her life when free of addiction.*

- Rites of Passage Passport (p.54)—Have the client create a passport of events and rites of passage he is looking forward to—the entire passport can be devoted to the stages of recovery and sobriety, or sobriety can be a page within the passport itself.

- Triptych (p.70)—Ask the client to create a triptych devoted to her journey toward sobriety.

  o The center panel can be a self-portrait and the side panels can be the influences that are aiding in her recovery and healing.

  o The center panel can be a self-portrait and the side panels can express how her life will be different when sober.

  o The panels can represent the past, present, and future of her journey through recovery.

- Journaling (p.81)—Ask the client to journal about five things he wants to accomplish before he turns 21.

- Wishes (p.90)—Have the client create a section in her journal on Wishes. Wishes can help a client define what they want in life, which also helps in establishing goals that are not substance-related.

- Freedom From (p.93)—Have the client journal how his life would look if he were free from addiction.

- Rites of Passage Plan (p.95):

    o Have the client create a plan for how she is going to commemorate and celebrate her successes along the road to sobriety.

    o It is equally important for the client to plan ahead for mistakes and failures along the way as well. Help the client prepare for these moments so that she has a plan in place to get back on the right path toward sobriety again.

GOAL: The client will create an alternate coping plan that does not involve using substances.

- Personal Mantras (p.46)—Work with the client to create a mantra he can turn to when he is feeling like using. For example, if the client feels the urge to use a substance, he can focus on the mantra word to help distract and re-focus.

- Refer to section on Mood Disorders, Anxiety Disorders, and General Coping Skills (p.116) for alternate coping plan strategies.

GOAL: The client will address how friendships are affecting his/her substance usage and/or recovery.

- A Kaleidoscope of Friends (p.85)—Have the client journal about her current or recent friendships. Discuss how her friends can help or hinder her success in recovery.

Dissociative Disorders

♦ ♦ ♦ ♦ ♦ ♦ ♦ ♦ ♦ ♦ ♦ ♦ ♦ ♦ ♦ ♦ ♦ ♦ ♦

GOAL: The client will start to integrate his/her fractal personalities into one person.

- Me, Myself, and I—Three Building Blocks (p.24)—This activity can only be done if your client is aware of his other personalities, or is far enough along in treatment that he is working toward integration. The number of blocks used in this activity will actually be the number of personalities or fractals that your client has. Your client will need one wooden block per personality. Have your client decorate each block with information or pictures about that personality. For example, a block might have the name of the person; their favorite food; what their age is; and what their personality is typically like or the role they play. When all of the blocks are complete, they can be used as a visual tool for communicating about the personalities, e.g. how they are working together or split off from each other. Are the blocks scattered today or can they work together today to build something?

- Personal Mantras (p.46)—Have the client choose a word she can focus on when trying to stay integrated. If any of the personalities can communicate to each other, work with them, if possible, to support the client, e.g. fractal personalities may be able to remind your client to use her Personal Mantra.

- Mixed Media Self-Portraits (p.50)—Have the client create a self-portrait that includes all of his personalities that he is aware of. The use of multiple art mediums in this activity is conducive to representing multiple components of the self.

- A Kaleidoscope of Friends (p.85)—The client can journal about her multiple or fractal personalities in the same format as the Kaleidoscope of Friends activity. Have the client describe how each personality helps or hinders her in everyday life.

GOAL: The client will list situations (past and present) that trigger dissociative behavior.

- Life Map (p.33)—Have the client create a pirate map. Ask the client to use buried treasure chests to represent places in his life where he "buried" certain parts of his self, secrets, or memories.

- Secrets with Wings (p.44)—If your client has a history of trauma that is affecting her ability to integrate personalities, or feel "in her body," this activity may be a gentle way for her to start letting go of secrets about it.

GOAL: The client will keep an ongoing journal of his/her daily life to help monitor and keep track of his personalities.

- Photojournalism (p.23)—If the client enjoys photography, ask him to take photos of his daily life and create an ongoing album with these photos. The photos can help create a timeline of his daily experiences.

- Paper Chains (p.72)—Ask your client to create an ongoing paper chain of her daily experiences. Each link represents a day. This intervention may be especially appealing to those personalities that are younger. If younger personalities are not able to write, they can choose colors to represent feelings or draw pictures on the links.

- Journaling (p.81)—The client can keep an ongoing journal of daily activities and events. It may be helpful to pre-date the pages to help the client keep track of time and dates.

Gender Identity Disorders

♦ ♦ ♦ ♦ ♦ ♦ ♦ ♦ ♦ ♦ ♦ ♦ ♦ ♦ ♦ ♦ ♦ ♦

GOAL: The client will define and accept his/her gender identity.

- Photojournalism (p.23)—The client can create a photo journal of his transition from one gender to another, or his struggle with gender identity in general.

- Letter to Your Child Self (p.42)—Have the client write a letter to her child self telling her what she needed to hear from an older person or mentor at that stage of life.

- Secrets with Wings (p.44)—If the client has not disclosed to his family or public about his gender identity, have him create a piece of art that portrays what it's like for him to have this secret. He could also create a piece of artwork that has his "secret" somewhere hidden in it as a way to "get it out" and release it in treatment.

- Mixed Media Self-Portraits (p.50)—Assign the client to create a self-portrait in which her gender identity is expressed or represented. For example, a client might represent the male and female aspects of her own self. Or, a client might express her gender identity with a 3-D portrait of a male within a female body or vice versa.

- Mini Graphic Novels (p.88)—Have your client create some graphic novel stories about his struggle with gender identity.

- Wishes (p.90)—Ask your client to write a journal entry about what her life would look and feel like if her wish to be the other gender came true. What other wishes does your client have about her gender that she can discuss or write about?

• Freedom From (p.93)—Have the client write a journal entry about how his life would be different if he were born a different gender; if society was more comfortable coping with gender fluidity; or if the client were the gender he desires.

GOAL: The client will create a coping/strategy plan for "coming out" or changing gender identities.

• Rites of Passage Passport (p.54)—Ask the client to create a Rite of Passage Passport about the life experiences she is looking forward to when she can live the gender or identity she desires.

• Rites of Passage Plan (p.95)—Work with your client to create a plan that prepares him for both the celebratory and challenging aspects of this life decision he is facing.

Adjustment Disorders and Grief

◆ ◆ ◆ ◆ ◆ ◆ ◆ ◆ ◆ ◆ ◆ ◆ ◆ ◆ ◆ ◆ ◆ ◆

GOAL: The client will create a coping plan for managing difficult life moments and/or transitions.

- Coping strategies from the section on Mood Disorders, Anxiety Disorders, and General Coping Skills (p.116) can be used in the client's coping plan.

- Personal Mantras (p.46)—Have the client create a mantra or word he can focus on when he is feeling distress about changes or transitions. For example, "Breathe"; "This too shall pass"; "Relax"; "Calm"; or "I can do this."

- Inspiration Decks (p.66)—The client can create a deck of cards to remind her of different coping strategies or words of comfort. When she is feeling distraught, she can choose a card from her deck for added support or reminding.

- Rites of Passage Plan (p.95)—Help your client plan ahead for transitions (including losses) in his life by creating a Rites of Passage Plan.

GOAL: To facilitate the grieving process, the client will create a piece of artwork that pays tribute to the memory of _____.

- Altered Books (p.20)—Ask the client to create a memory book or scrapbook about this loss or transition in her life.

- Photojournalism (p.23)—Have the client create a photo journal that pays tribute to the life he just left behind, or a photo journal of memories shared with the person that has passed away.

- Mini Shrines (p.35)—If the client is having trouble adjusting to life after the loss of a loved one, have her create a Mini Shrine in memory of the person.

- Shadowboxing (p.61)—The client can create a Shadowbox in memory of a person, place or pet. For example, here are some items that might go into a Shadowbox collection in memory of a pet dog that has passed away:

  ○ the dog's license tag

  ○ the dog's name tag

  ○ a part of the dog's collar

  ○ a favorite dog toy (or a picture or other representation of it)

  ○ a favorite photo of the dog

  ○ any charms that remind the client of his dog, e.g. a dog biscuit charm; a fire hydrant charm

  ○ a miniature stick.

- Triptychs (p.70)—Have the client create a memorial triptych about her loss. The central panel can have a photo or drawing of the person or pet that has passed away. The side panels can include written memories; pictures and photos that remind her of happy moments with them; or collage items from special moments with that person or pet, such as a movie ticket stub or a piece of paper from the dog's adoption papers.

- Paper Chains (p.72)—Your client can create a paper chain made of links that have memories written on them. If you do any group work with teenagers, you can also create a paper chain of collected memories from the group. This activity may be especially helpful if the group of teens have lost a teacher or a classmate.

- Tribute to a Special Memory (p.78)—Help your client put together and assemble a collection of items that honor the client's loss or major life change. Clients can create these tributes for many occasions, including:

  o After a home has burned—Photos of the house; written memories about the house; any small salvaged items from the fire; and newspaper articles about the fire can be added to a tribute.

  o After a move to a new school—Many times our clients have cards and notes from the former class saying goodbye. These can be included in a tribute along with any school work from the school (e.g. a good grade cut out from a completed homework assignment); class photos; a client's drawing or photos of friends from the previous school; any small items that may have the former school's logo on it.

  o Changes in foster homes—If the client had a positive experience spending time with a foster family, he can create a tribute to this time of his life. This can be a nice activity for the foster family and teen to complete together for closure, if at all possible. Any mementos from their time together can be included, such as tickets to events or a new recipe the teen enjoyed while there. Other memorable items can be included as well—a small token from the home as a transitional object; a photo of the family; or a drawing from a younger foster sibling.

- Snapshot Moments (p.86)—Ask the client to journal about Snapshot Moments she experienced regarding the life change or loss.

Trauma

◆ ◆ ◆ ◆ ◆ ◆ ◆ ◆ ◆ ◆ ◆ ◆ ◆ ◆ ◆ ◆ ◆ ◆ ◆ ◆

GOAL: The client will create a plan to address sleep disturbances.

- Personal Mantras (p.46)—Have the client choose a calming word she can think about at bedtime to relax and quiet the mind. If it's helpful for her, have her create a piece of art with her mantra. The client can hang this piece of art near her bed for support at sleep time. Some calming sleep words include "Rest"; "Sleep"; "Slumber"; "Peace."

- Recurring Dreams (p.58)—If your client is experiencing recurring dreams after a traumatic event, it may be helpful for him to create a piece of art about it. It can be quite difficult for some people to express or define the details of such dreams and memories verbally.

GOAL: The client will verbalize his/her trauma experience and her feelings about it.

- Me, Myself, and I—Three Building Blocks (p.24)— Challenge the client to use building blocks as a medium for expressing her emotions around the trauma. The three building blocks could represent life before the trauma; life in the midst of trauma; and her path to healing. The blocks could also represent her personal strengths that helped her survive the trauma.

- Life Map (p.33)—Have the client create a Life Map that shows a representation of the trauma somewhere within the map. The trauma can be coded as a color, a symbol, or a metaphor on the map.

- A Tribute to Imaginary Friends (p.38)—If your client experienced trauma as a child and had imaginary friends that he used to help him get through it, have him create an artistic tribute to these imaginary friends.

- Letter to Your Child Self (p.42)—If the trauma happened to the client as a child, she could write a letter to her child self as the teen she is now. She could let her child self know some strategies to help heal through the trauma, such as using personal strengths, coping skills, natural supports, and words of wisdom.

- Secrets with Wings (p.44)—There may be aspects to a traumatic experience that your client has difficulty articulating or "telling." If this is the case, assign him to show, express, or represent the trauma in an artistic work. The trauma can be represented metaphorically (as a color, symbol, or combination of images) or literally (i.e. written).

- Emo Dolls (p.56)—Ask the client to create a single doll or a series of dolls that express her feelings around the trauma.

- Freedom From (p.93)—Have the client journal about what his life will look like when he has healed and moved beyond the trauma.

Creative Coping Skills for Children

Emotional Support through Arts and Crafts Activities

Bonnie Thomas

ISBN 9781843109211

Paperback: £18.99/$29.95

'Bonnie Thomas' new book *Creative Coping Skills for Children – Emotional Support Through Arts and Crafts Activities* (2009) is a goldmine of helpful and simple arts and crafts based activities that are designed to show children how to cope with their emotions.'

— *Brighthub.com (9th September 2009)*

Everyone has different needs when it comes to coping with life's stressors, and children are no different. Some need quiet and soothing activities to calm them down, whereas others require more physical activity or intense sensory input to relax their minds and bodies.

This resource comprises a collection of fun, flexible, tried-and-tested activities, and make-it-yourself workbooks for parents and professionals to help a child in need of extra emotional support find the coping skills that fit them best. Each activity lists the materials required and includes clear directions for how to do it. There is something for every child: whether they are dynamic and creative or more cerebral and literal. Projects include making wish fairies, dream catchers, and mandalas; managing unstructured time with activities such as creating comics, dioramas, and tongue twisters; and simple ideas for instant soothing, such as taking deep breaths, blowing bubbles, making silly faces, and playing music. *Creative Coping Skills for Children* also includes specific interventions for anxious or grieving children such as making worry dolls and memory shrines.

This book is full of fun, easy, creative project ideas for parents of children aged 3–12, teachers, counselors, play therapists, social workers, and all professionals working with children.

Arts Activities for Children and Young People in Need

Helping Children to Develop Mindfulness, Spiritual Awareness and Self-Esteem

Diana Coholic

ISBN 9781849050012

Paperback: £19.99/$32.95

Art-based activities can develop resilience and self-esteem, enabling children in need to cope better with ongoing stress and loss. *Arts Activities for Children and Young People in Need* offers interventions and exercises drawn from practice and research, for practitioners to use as a basis for their own arts-based groups or one-to-one sessions.

Holistic arts activities facilitate a spiritually sensitive approach. Mindfulness-based exercises underpin the approach, and include guided meditations in which a group imagines that they are clouds, or draw feelings and emotions while listening to music, to encourage awareness of the senses. The activities help the group to relax and become more self-aware, encourage an exploration of feelings, values and understanding and are beneficial for children not ready to embrace traditional therapies or counselling.

This book is accessible and suitable for helping, health and education practitioners and students from a variety of disciplines, such as social work, psychology and counselling.

Diana Coholic is Associate Professor in the School of Social Work at Laurentian University, Canada. Her research programme studies the effectiveness of holistic arts-based methods with children who have significant problems. She has been a social work practitioner for 18 years, and also maintains a small private practice working with children and young people.

Children and Adolescents in Trauma
Creative Therapeutic Approaches

Edited by Chris Nicholson, Michael Irwin and Kedar Nath Dwivedi

Foreword by Peter Wilson

ISBN 9781843104377

Paperback £22.99/$34.95

Part of the Community, Culture and Change series

'A worthwhile read for all counselling practitioners and a very useful overview for those starting out.'

– Therapy Today, *Cicely Gill, Counsellor*

Children and Adolescents in Trauma presents a variety of creative approaches to working with young people in residential children's homes, secure or psychiatric units, and special schools.

The contributors describe a wide range of approaches, including art therapy and literature, and how creative methods are applied in cases of abuse, trauma, violence, self-harm and identity development. They discuss the impact of abuse and mistreatment upon the mental health of 'looked after' children, drawing links between psychoanalytic theory and practice and the study of literature and the arts.

This indispensable book provides useful insights and a fresh perspective for anyone working with traumatised children and adolescents, including social workers, psychotherapists, arts therapists, psychiatrists, counsellors, psychologists and students in these fields.

Chris Nicholson PhD is a Lecturer in the Centre for Psychoanalytic Studies at the University of Essex. Formerly Therapeutic Services Manager at Donyland Lodge, a therapeutic community in Colchester, he has worked in a range of children's services for over 10 years. Chris is a Trustee of the Charterhouse Group of Therapeutic Communities and a Fellow of the International Institute of Child and Adolescent Mental Health. **Michael Irwin** MA, BLit, is Emeritus Professor of English at the University of Kent. Apart from his academic work, he has also published two novels and written or translated several opera libretti. **Dr Kedar Nath Dwivedi** MBBS, MD, DPM, FRCPsych, is a Visiting Professor at the London Metropolitan University and Director of the International Institute of Child and Adolescent Mental Health. Formerly, he served as a Consultant Child Psychiatrist at Northampton General Hospital and has edited or co-edited several books.

Contemporary Art Therapy with Adolescents

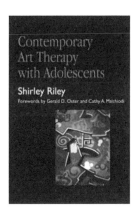

Shirley Riley

Foreword by Gerald D. Oster and Cathy Malchiodi

ISBN 9781853026379

Paperback £19.95/$31.95

Contemporary Art Therapy with Adolescents offers practical and imaginative solutions to the multifaceted challenges that clinicians face when treating young people. The author fuses the contemporary theories of clinical treatment with the creative processes of art therapy to arrive at a synthesis which yields successful outcomes when working with adolescents. Clinicians of allied disciplines, particularly art therapists, will find practical suggestions for using imagery to enrich their relationships with teenaged clients. The process of using art-making therapeutically and the challenges of applying creativity in the current mental health world are explored.

Shirley Riley reviews current theories on adolescent development and therapy, and emphasizes the primary importance of relying on the youths' own narrative in the context of their social and economic backgrounds. She has found this approach preferential to following pre-designed assessment directives as a primary function of art therapy. Family, group and individual treatment are examined, as is the adolescent's response to short- and long-term treatment in residential and therapeutic school settings. The book is firmly rooted in Riley's clinical experience of working with this age group, and her proven ability to combine contemporary theories of adolescent treatment with inventive and effective art expressions.

Shirley Riley (1931-2004) was a registered art therapist and a licensed marriage and family counsellor in private practice. She was a highly regarded educator and taught in university programmes in the United States, Europe and Asia. She received awards for her clinical skills and wrote many articles and books, for art therapy and allied professions.